P9-CFY-592

The Community of the Spirit

The Community
of
the Spirit

by
C. Norman Kraus

William B. Eerdmans Publishing Company
Grand Rapids, Michigan

Copyright © 1974 by Wm. B. Eerdmans Publishing Company
All rights reserved
Printed in the United States of America

Library of Congress Cataloging in Publication Data

Kraus, Clyde Norman.
  The community of the spirit.

  Includes bibliographical references.
1. Church. I. Title.
BV600.2.K68   262   74-1479
ISBN 0-8028-1562-6

262.73
K91

Wm. B. Eerdmans Pub. Co.

1. 17

19 Nov. 1974

Contents

51420

Preface

In the sixteenth century the Anabaptists represented a third voice in the debate between Protestant reformers and those who championed Roman Orthodoxy. During the past fifty years historians have done much to uncover the essential features of these more "radical" brothers, but few have joined the contemporary dialogue from the Anabaptist perspective. Arthur Gish's *The New Left and Christian Radicalism* and John Howard Yoder's *The Politics of Jesus* are two exceptions.

The biblically oriented Anabaptists were evangelical in the true and original sense of that word. They were the evangelistic movement of the sixteenth century. They called men and women to a life of discipleship, of brotherly sharing, love for enemies, and witness to the established order. Central for them was the idea that in the true visible church the believer was joined to Christ. They believed that Christians live in a new order and their vocation in the world is to obey Christ implicitly in whatever occupation they might find themselves.

The present essay does not pretend to defend the Anabaptists. They too were fallible. But what is attempted is a contemporary joining of pertinent issues in evangelical Christianity from an Anabaptist perspective. Spirit and law, faith and obedience, justification and regeneration, individual experience and life in community, church and world were all major areas of discussion then, and continue to be central although the specific shape of the issues has changed.

I have argued in this essay that what we need are some new models and definitions to help us move into the new historical situation that faces us. Like my Anabaptist forebears, I have tried to base these definitions and models squarely on Scripture. I offer this as a sketch, as a sign pointing in the right direction and not as a comprehensive, scholarly treatise.

C. Norman Kraus
Center for Discipleship
Goshen College
May 1973

CHAPTER ONE

Pentecost and the Gospel

The formation of the community of the Spirit at Pentecost in 33 A.D. is also part of the gospel. For many years now we have been told that the Christian gospel or good news is about the events which fulfilled the promises God had made through the prophets to Israel. The rather quaint King James phrase "and it came to pass" really puts it very well. The gospel actually happened! Jesus of Nazareth came as the promised Messiah and through his resurrection from the dead was "designated Son of God with power by the Holy Spirit" (Rom. 1:3-4). What has not been said with equal clarity and conviction is that the events of that first Christian Pentecost were a part of this incarnation drama.

The word *gospel* has come to have distinctly religious connotations. No one calls it gospel when he receives the good news of a raise in salary or of a long-awaited vacation. These are nonreligious events belonging to everyday life, which we sometimes refer to as secular (from the Latin meaning "this age"). At the time the New Testament was written, however, the word we have translated gospel referred to just that kind of "hard news," as the modern news reporter would say. On the day of Pentecost Peter told the crowds that it was what Jesus had done publicly ("in your midst as you yourselves know") during his ministry that had convinced them that he was from God. "Gospel" is different

9

from doctrine, or exhortation, or theory, or belief. It announces an event.

The specific shape of the good news in the Christian tradition is the announcement that what was long promised and expected has now happened. Promise has become reality. That is the fundamental message of the New Testament. The good news is not that there is *more to come in the future,* heaven or an earthly kingdom for example. It is not that if one believes hard enough, *faith will make it so.* It is not that the *correct philosophical formula* has been found to demonstrate that "God is there" after all, although in fact that may be the case. Neither is it that a *new ethical principle of agape* (love) has been given to free men from the tyranny of legalism.

The gospel is that the promised "power of God for salvation" (Rom. 1:16) has become reality for all who have eyes to see and ears to hear! Of course, there are those who still have not heard or will not hear the news. But the gospel proclaims a present reality. That is of the essence.

The gospel announces both something which happened in the past and something which is happening in the present. The story begins with what happened when Jesus the Christ initiated a new chapter in the history of humanity. He came announcing that "the rule of God" (this is more nearly the meaning of the phrase than "kingdom of God") was about to begin, and his ministry actually initiated it. That happened many years ago; but if it is truly good news for mankind in the twentieth century, then there must be something happening in the present tense also! Further, if what happened in the past is really part of the gospel, it must have a demonstrable relation to the present reality.

The relation of a past event to the present is, indeed, a crucial problem, and the earliest Christians already faced it. After all, the past is past whether it be four days, forty days, forty years, or forty centuries. Yesterday is memory. Today is reality. The days immediately following the crucifixion were some of the darkest! The disciples were in despair because all their experiences, all their present realities with Jesus, and all their hope for the future were suddenly a memory.

When they learned that Jesus was alive on the third day, their *hopes* for the *future* were revived. Now he might yet bring in the kingdom which he had initiated. But what of *present* reality? At first they found it difficult even to ask the question about the present. Their minds jumped to a future near or far when he would "restore the kingdom to Israel." But the good news that Jesus came preaching was that the promise is already a significant reality in the present time, and not that fulfillment is now more certain even though postponed to an unknown future.

The genius of New Testament Christianity is that gospel is interpreted neither in terms of a legacy from the past nor as a new certainty for future fulfillment. The good news is that the promise has been fulfilled; hope is realized. In a profound new way God's presence and power are a *now* reality to accomplish His will on earth. Not, of course, that a future culmination is denied; but the problem has been that a preoccupation with future reality has undercut present expectation and possibility.

What happened at Pentecost provides the connecting link between past and present. The continuity between the historical presence of Jesus and our present salvation was disclosed in the living presence of the Spirit of Christ. At Pentecost Christ became a dynamic contemporary reality never again to be absent from his disciples.[1] As Martin Luther once put it, the Spirit is the true *vicar* (authoritative presence) of Christ, and not some religious institutional representative which preserves Christ's legacy in his absence.

The Meaning of Pentecost

Pentecost as it is reported in the Acts is the climax of the three-act drama of incarnation. Act one presents

---

1. Donald Baillie has developed this point in a most insightful way in his *God Was in Christ,* Scribners, 1948, pp. 153-54.

various scenes in the ministry of Jesus. Act two is the passion of the Christ. Act three is the triumphant advance of the victorious Lord. At Pentecost "the promise of the Father" was fulfilled (Luke 24:49 and Acts 1:4). The ministry, death, and resurrection were not the completion of the promise. That is why Jesus told his followers to wait in Jerusalem. "Jerusalem" was the point of departure for the triumphant mission — "beginning at Jerusalem" (Luke 24:48) — and they were to "sit tight" (*kathisate*) until the promise had become full reality. It was not simply a matter of their receiving an individual spiritual capability for service and witness to what Christ had already finished. No, they were not to begin their mission because the Father had not yet completed the formation of the new body through which the Christ would continue and expand his presence and ministry.[2]

The drama of incarnation does not conclude with a final act that neatly wraps up the loose ends of the story and draws the curtain. Rather it ends with an open future for those involved. Pentecost is a commencement in the same sense that we use the word to describe a graduation. It is simultaneously climax and beginning.[3] It concludes with the assurance that this is not the end but the beginning. Christ is not dead or absent in some far-off spiritual realm. The kingdom he announced is not set aside to some future millennium but enters a new era of fulfillment. His ministry is not concluded but universalized through his new body.[4] Surely this is part of the good news!

It is difficult to believe that Luke did not intentionally use parallel language when he spoke of the Spirit's work

2. F. D. Bruner has a splendid discussion of this passage, but as usual he is aiming pietistic guns at pentecostal positions and fails to consider that more than personal enduement is at stake. See *A Theology of the Holy Spirit*, Eerdmans, 1970, pp. 155ff.

3. G. S. H. Lampe speaks of Pentecost as "the great turning point in history" (p. 192). See his "The Holy Spirit in the Writings of St. Luke," in *Studies in the Gospels*, edited by D. E. Nineham, Oxford, 1955, pp. 159-200.

4. Donald Baillie, *op. cit.*, pp. 145-46.

in preparing the human body of the historical Messiah and in preparing a new human body for the resurrected Lord. According to his account the angel told Mary, "the Holy Spirit *will come upon you,* and the *power* of the Most High will overshadow you..." (Luke 1:35). In Acts 1:8 Jesus told his disciples, "You shall receive *power* when the Holy Spirit *has come upon you....*" In both cases the body of Christ is to be formed through a special work of God's Spirit. This is obviously incarnational language and strongly suggests the closest kind of association between the ministry of Jesus, which was in a unique way the work of the Spirit (Luke 3:22; 4:1, 18), and the ministry of the church. That the Christ is still present and at work among men in an earthly body is an integral part of the good news.

The continuity between the ministry of Jesus in his incarnation and the mission of the apostles is also indicated by Luke in his report of the discussion between the resurrected Jesus and his disciples. The disciples' talk continued to be about the "gospel of the kingdom of God" (Acts 1:3), and they still did not grasp the true nature of the rule of God which Jesus came to inaugurate. They still viewed it as the restoration of national autonomy to Israel with a political Messiah. They were still thinking of the kingdom in terms of political power. Jesus brushed aside their misconceived question about "times and seasons" and spoke of the kingdom in terms of the power of God at work among men. He associated the presence of the kingdom with the promised power of the Holy Spirit which would be theirs to fulfill his mission.

This was the same word he had spoken during his pre-resurrection ministry. In Matthew 12:28, for example, he identified the presence of the kingdom or rule of God with the power of the Holy Spirit casting out demons. In other contexts he pointed to God's power to heal, to establish righteousness, and to accomplish his will on earth as signs or evidences of his rule.

We conclude then that the gospel and salvation of which Jesus and his apostles spoke included the events of Pentecost. In these events the promise became a continuing reality. The mission which Jesus inaugurated in his earthly ministry was continued through the presence of his Spirit in his new body. This is indeed good news!

What Really Happened?

What *really* happened at Pentecost? This question now becomes crucial, for Pentecost is part of the gospel. The question has been asked and answered by many commentators and theologians, but it has seldom been asked in this context.

The answers have largely focused on the manifestations that caught the attention of the puzzled onlookers. Did the reported phenomena *literally* happen or not? When asked this way, the question is put into a twentieth-century, Western context. "Really" is interpreted as "literally" or "empirically." What did the crowds see and hear? The questions usually continue in the same vein: Should we expect a literal recurrence of such manifestations today? How and when do individuals receive the Spirit? Such questions are intriguing and important for some purposes, but to make them the central concern is to remain in the company of the onlookers!

Luke himself makes clear what he understood to be of central importance in the account. He does this both by the language he uses and by the way he constructs the account. His summaries in 2:43-47 and 4:32-37 highlight preceding developments and act as a bridge to the next sections of the story. These summaries indicate clearly what Luke thought had really happened. Further, just as there are parallelisms between the birth, life, and ministry of Jesus *(Luke)* and the church *(Acts)* so there are in both accounts fairly obvious allusions and parallelisms with the story of the exodus and formation of Israel into a people of God.[5] Both of these

---

5. See Maurice Barnett, *The Living Flame*, Epworth Press, 1953; Otto Piper, "Exodus in the New Testament," *Interpretation* (January, 1957), pp. 3-22; and Harold Sahlin, "The New Exodus of Salva-

literary devices indicate the same answer to our question. *What really happened at Pentecost was the forming of the new covenant community of the Spirit.* Let us look more closely at the significance of these characteristics of Luke's account.

The teaching that the church was born at Pentecost is, of course, not new. Nor is the idea of continuity as well as discontinuity with Israel new, although this has been a matter of dispute within evangelicalism. What has not been sufficiently recognized is that the new thing that happened on Pentecost *is the new community.* It is this parallelism with the formation of Israel from a "mixed multitude" into a "people" that Luke's many allusions to *Exodus* seem to underscore.

The immediate manifestations of the Spirit's presence were fire, wind, and speaking in other tongues. All three have a rich and varied symbolic use in the Old Testament and other Jewish literature. No doubt Luke consciously alludes to this tradition. To make exodus symbolism primary is not to rule out all other possible allusions, but rather to highlight the fundamental significance in his account.

As the Israelites left Egypt the special presence of the Lord leading his people was manifested in the "pillar of fire" (Exod. 13:21-22; 14:24). Now that presence appears again and disperses itself, resting on each one in the representative new Israel (Acts 2:3). The mysterious "violent wind" which dried up the waters of the Red Sea (Exod. 14:21) and whipped in the faces of the Israelites as they crossed to Sinai now again filled the house with a roar and is fully identified as God's Spirit. The play on words in the original languages of the Bible makes this more obvious. Both *ruach* (Hebrew) and *pneuma* (Greek) have the double meaning of wind and spirit. There are also other words for wind that do not have the double meaning. These other words occur in the *Septuagint* account of the wind *(anemos)* drying up the Red Sea and also in some places

tion According to St. Paul," in *The Root of the Vine,* edited by Anton Fridrichsen, Philosophical Library, 1953, pp. 81ff.

in the Acts 2 account of the rushing wind *(pnoe)* at Pentecost. But the original texts make it plain that the *anemos* of Exodus and the *pnoe* of Acts are in fact the *pneuma* of God!

The symbolism of speaking and hearing in different dialects is also multifaceted. It most likely alludes to the confusion of languages at Babel (Gen. 11:7-9). The Spirit's presence reverses Babel, and as St. Paul said, in Christ there are no "barbarians," i.e., those of uncouth languages (Col. 3:11). It also indicates the universality of the salvation message and therefore the mission and nature of the new people being formed. The connection with *Exodus* and Sinai is not so apparent until we learn that there was a Jewish tradition that the Mosaic Law had been given in seventy languages simultaneously, indicating the universal scope of its authority. Luke's account of the new covenant's being announced in many languages may well be a parallel to this Jewish tradition "about the marvelous manifestation of divine power that accompanied the giving of the law at Sinai."[6]

In his sermon Peter explained all this as the fulfillment of Joel's prophecy. Jesus, the true Messiah, has sealed the new covenant in his death. Now risen and victorious he is forming his new people. Just as the Israelites were "baptized in the sea" (I Cor. 10:2), marking decisively their separation from their old family identity in Egypt, so Peter called upon his audience to be baptized and to save themselves from the old "crooked nation" *(genea)*. Just as Israel received their new identity as the people of God at Sinai through the *gift of the Law*, so the new people is constituted through the *gift to the Spirit*. And just as great signs accompanied Israel's deliverance and formation into a covenant nation, so "signs and wonders done through the apostles" accompanied the birth of the new community of the Spirit.

---

6. Howard Kee, Franklin Young, and Karlfried Froelich, *Understanding the New Testament*, Prentice Hall, 1965, p. 306. Although the written rabbinic source of this tradition is later than the *Acts* account, it may well have been oral tradition prior to that. At any rate, it gives an authentic clue to the symbolism.

The Legacy of Evangelicalism

The interpretation of Pentecost which I have offered differs in several significant aspects from the usual pentecostal or fundamentalist interpretations. It will help us to see where the significant issues lie if we digress a moment in order to put what has been said into historical perspective. The "standard" interpretations offered in evangelicalism are definitely linked to historical developments as well as to logical deductions and biblical linguistics.

Modern evangelicalism is the heir of seventeenth-century Protestant orthodoxy, which focused its attention upon the doctrines of an objective atonement and justification by faith in the "finished work of Christ." Reacting against the vagaries of "spiritualism," the Protestant tradition also laid great stress upon Scripture as the touchstone for any claims to Spirit guidance or enlightenment. Neither the Reformed nor Lutheran orthodoxy had much to say about the gift of the Spirit and the implications of this gift for the life of the church. Having accepted the basic assumptions and definitions of this theological tradition, modern evangelicalism has never come to grips in a concerted way with the full significance of the gospel of Pentecost. Let me explain.

Contemporary American evangelicalism is broadly divided into three schools of interpretation on the question of Pentecost and the work of the Holy Spirit. Two of these, which I shall refer to as *pentecostal* and *pietistic,* stand in the sharpest contrast. The orthodox pietistic tradition, which is often referred to as fundamentalism, has been reluctantly tolerant of the *holiness* tradition in its Wesleyan and Keswick expressions, although basic differences and theological tensions still exist.

Pietism arose in the latter sixteenth and early seventeenth centuries as a renewal movement within the establishd Lutheran and Reformed churches. The Pietists were deeply concerned to correct the formalism, intellectualism, and lack of personal involvement in the established churches. This concern led them to stress individual piety and experience. They accepted the established Protestant institutions within which they were operating as valid reformed churches but deplored their lack of true spirituality and worked for individual renewal and authenticity.

In this situation they interpreted the pentecostal experience as one of individual renewal (conversion in contrast to profession) and preparation for holy living. They did not visualize its outcome as primarily a new corporate reality — a new body or church indwelled by the Holy Spirit. For them the mark of the authentic visible church was orthodoxy in word and sacrament. Their "conventicles" were societies for mutual religious discipline and fellowship which added warmth and spiritual depth to orthodoxy.[7] Although the notion that members of these "little churches within the church" were the true church was latent and implicit, it was not given explicit expression in their theology of the Spirit.

The precise character of the conventicle depended on the relative importance attached to *feeling* (experience of the Spirit's presence and power) on the one hand or to *faith* as an act of the intellect and will on the other. An emphasis on experience stimulated fellowship and an open expression of the Spirit's "gifts." A stress on faith tended to produce groups for the spiritual discipline of Bible study, prayer and moral living. In this difference were the seeds of future dissension and divisions.

The Wesleyan wing of Pietism stressed the "felt Christ" (a term from Whitefield) and holiness.[8] Although Wesley fully acknowledged the Spirit's work in conversion, he placed more emphasis on the "second work" of sanctification and motivation for holy living. In time this emphasis on the special continuing work of the Holy Spirit opened the way for experiencing the "gifts" of the Spirit. These gifts were given not

---

7. Ernest Stoeffler says that they were attempting to "capture the meaning of the early Koinonia." See *The Rise of Evangelical Pietism*, Brill, 1965, p. 160.

8. Lycurgus Starkey has given an excellent exposition of this type of theology and experience in his *The Work of the Holy Spirit: A Study in Wesleyan Theology*, Abingdon, 1962.

only for assurance and to lift everyday life to a higher plane, but for special guidance, healing, and power in witnessing.

In contrast to the holiness emphasis, which incidentally tended toward an Arminian theological assumption, the more orthodox (Calvinistic) Pietists insisted that the special gifts of the Spirit were a strictly New Testament phenomenon that ceased with the apostolic generation.[9] They were part of the initial revelation like miracles and signs which the apostles performed to validate the message. These pietistic evangelicals continued a modified Calvinistic position, maintaining the doctrines of salvation by God's election and the eternal security of believers. Evidence of election was given through an inner assurance and change of attitude, not by outward experiences. They insisted that believers received the Holy Spirit when they "accepted Christ." The Spirit's "filling" was to be accepted *by faith* and not on the basis of some special experience or manifestation of gifts.

A third variant in American evangelicalism arose in the late nineteenth and early twentieth century and chose the name Pentecostalism.[10] This movement muted sanctification as the dominant work of the Spirit and accentuated the ecstatic, emotional aspects of experience in a "baptism of the Spirit and of fire!" In a very literal way it reintroduced the gifts of tongues, prophecy, healing, and other works of "faith" as signs of the Spirit's presence and baptism.

All three of these positions continue within evangelicalism. The differences are most pronounced in the rift between the pentecostal and pietistic wings. These differences have been obvious and in some cases explosive, but what has been overlooked are the significant agreements and shared assumptions of the two movements. Both groups begin with the same individualistic

---

9. See B. B. Warfield, "The Cessation of the Charismata," in *Miracles: Yesterday and Today, True and False,* Eerdmans, 1953, pp. 1-32.
10. Vinson Synan has made this distinction very clear in his *The Holiness Pentecostal Movement,* Eerdmans, 1971.

definition of salvation. Both interpret Pentecost as incidental to a salvation which is based upon the death and resurrection of Christ alone. Both view the experience of the outpouring of the Spirit as the private experience of an aggregate of saved individuals. Pentecost is not an essential part of their gospel of salvation.

Neither the pentecostal nor the pietistic wing of modern American evangelicalism has recognized the centrality of the community of the Spirit. Both have viewed the gift of the Spirit as essentially an individual experience. Pentecostals have stressed the importance of the ecstatic manifestations as signs to the believer. The Pietists have stressed the inner resources which the filling of the Spirit provides for personal piety and witness. Neither has seen that the fundamental work of the Spirit at Pentecost was the *formation of the new community itself*. Perhaps a new perspective on the central meaning of Pentecost is needed to help us surmount and resolve the old conflict which has been created in part by the very inadequacy of categories used by both sides.

Community and Individual

The interrelation of individual and community and the new significance of the individual in the new covenant are at the heart of what happened at Pentecost. There is a sense in which the individual acquires new prominence in the Pentecost story and in the New Testament as a whole. One of the genuinely new aspects of the community of the Spirit is that it is a community made up of "Spirit-filled" individuals. Indeed, the very notion of a community constituted by a "baptism of the Spirit" in contrast to law implies a new range and depth to individuality.

This new appreciation for and focus on the individual person is symbolized in the dispersion of the fire of God's presence into individual tongues of flame. Joel the prophet, whom Peter cites, had prophesied this surprising new personalizing of the gift of the Spirit across all class lines and distinctions. Jeremiah also foresaw the new covenant that would be written on each person's heart so that everyone in the new brotherhood would share individually in the knowledge of the Lord (Jer. 31:31-34). Peter's call to repent and be baptized is an appeal to individuals to change their allegiance. Crowds do not repent; individuals do.

This new element in the account is highly significant and must not be lost sight of. However, the dominance of the principle of "justification by faith" has diverted Protestant theologians from the original import of this new disclosure of individual dignity and freedom in Christian community. Luther's formulation of the polarity of law and grace, which became the standard Protestant category for biblical interpretation, obscured the even more elemental polarity of law and Spirit in Protestant interpretations of Pentecost.[11] The significance of the individual as it becomes manifest at Pentecost cannot best be understood as a transition from law and institutional bondage to the freedom of grace in which the individual experiences an immediate and essentially private justification by faith. At Pentecost persons who were "born under law," i.e., were members of a community of law, were called to become part of the new community of the Spirit. The fundamental difference between the old and new covenants is the shift from Torah (law) to Spirit as the formative basis of community. What is involved here, then, is the relation of Torah and Spirit and only secondarily law and grace.

The significance of this becomes clearer when we examine the relation of law and individuality. Law is for the regulation of societal activity, for the sake of the group. By definition it subjects the individual to the group in order to preserve the cohesiveness of the com-

---

11. The theologians of the Reformation worked with the opposing categories of *Bible* and *Spirit*, *law* and *grace*. Even the Anabaptist leaders by and large accepted these categories of Luther. Consequently in their stress upon conversion and the new life, they tended toward biblical literalism and the interpretation of the New Testament as a new law which by the grace of God can and should be obeyed. Calvin's biblicism and reinforcement of the Spirit's motivation with institutional sanctions is well attested.

munity. As a regulatory social institution it must of necessity be stated as nearly as possible in universal terms which can be uniformly applied and enforced. Thus law by its very nature generalizes and inhibits individual expression in favor of the group. From the vantage point of individual development, the best statute is one stated in the negative which can be uniformly interpreted, applied, and enforced while still leaving the greatest scope for positive action. But where there is no inner dynamic and motivation even the best law is impotent to effect what it prescribes or prevent what it prohibits.

To compensate for these handicaps and to keep the Jewish community intact, the scribal tradition which was developed from the time of Ezra expanded the prescriptions of Torah. Pharisaism was one of the highest types of legal religion and morality ever achieved in the ancient world, and it was developed during a period when the Jews commonly assumed that the Spirit of prophecy had been withdrawn. They had concluded that the religious community would have to be preserved by legal regulation and tradition. In the time of Jesus and the apostles, the Pharisaic community had expanded Torah into a comprehensive system of both prohibitive and prescriptive statutes, and it is this particular community of law that provides the background for Jesus and his apostles.

Jesus found himself in sharp conflict with this scribal tradition. In contrast to the scribes' legal authority, he was the bearer and dispenser of the Spirit, who, he promised, would lead his followers into all truth. While he respected and used the "law and the prophets," he did not construct a new religious system by developing their implications in some logical, or casuistical, way. For him "the Sabbath [law] was made for man and not man for the Sabbath." The "new commandment" which he left was not simply different in intention from the Mosaic covenant, but new in kind *(kaine)*. It was new precisely in the sense that it was not a legal statute.

His community would be constituted not by his new law but by his presence!

American Protestantism in both its liberal and conservative traditions has failed to catch the significance of the new community of the Spirit inaugurated by Jesus. Following the political model of John Locke's "social contract" (the term "social contract" actually comes from Rousseau), it has viewed the church as a voluntary society formed by a contractual ("covenant" in religious circles) arrangement between individuals who share commitments and goals. The contract, as with Locke, was essentially legal and functioned to preserve the freedom of the individual as much as the identity of the group.[12] Our social definitions and presuppositions inherited from the previous century have largely blinded us to the reality and dynamics of an organic or spiritual community, and it is precisely such a community which is designated *church* in the New Testament. Thus we fail to understand how the church can be the matrix for developing individuality and freedom in Christ.

Modern insights from anthropology, sociology, and psychology confirm the biblical presupposition that the basic human unit is not the independent individual before God but the *individual-in-community* before God. We become self-conscious individuals only in the process of community relationships. Indeed, we might say that personhood is the gift of the familial community. Thus the essential character and structure of community is integrally involved in the individual's self-identity. The nature of his responsibility and freedom is defined by the nature of his community. When we view the formation of the community of the Spirit at Pentecost from this perspective, we begin to appreciate

---

12. Sidney Meade has given us a most insightful analysis of the character of the American Protestant denomination in his book *The Lively Experiment, The Shaping of Christianity in America,* Harper and Row, 1963. See especially chapter VII, pp. 103ff. Welch, *The Reality of the Church,* Scribners, 1958, pages 31ff. refers to the Protestant notion of the church as a "voluntaristic association" and points out that it was characteristic of conservative and liberal alike.

its profound significance for the enhancement of individual spiritual attainment.

The biblical concept of individual-in-community as the basic unit of personal existence everywhere dominates the account of the first Christian Pentecost. The setting is a religious festival where Jews of the dispersion have gathered to celebrate their national identity and cohesion. During the festival these celebrants are called to reject their allegiance to the old religious community and openly identify with a new Messianic community in which the main feature is the Holy Spirit's renewed presence with God's people. This is the meaning of "repent and be baptized.... Save yourselves from this crooked generation" (Acts 2:38-40).

The story begins with the one hundred twenty disciples "all together in one place." When Peter is presented as spokesman, he is "standing with the eleven," and he appeals to the witness of the group to substantiate what he is saying. The crowd responds to "Peter and the rest of the apostles." The summary which follows accents the unity and fellowship of the new community. The new group was made up, to be sure, of individuals — redeemed, freed, and Spirit-filled individuals — but *individuals-in-koinonia*. It was precisely this new fellowship of the Spirit that so impressed "all the people."

On the day of Pentecost, to be saved meant to join the Messianic (later called the Christian) community. On that day baptism in the name of Jesus Christ was a public act of acknowledging that Jesus was truly the Messiah, the rightful leader of God's people, and a declaration of allegiance to him *by throwing in one's lot* with the original apostolic band. To be as explicit as possible let me perhaps overstate the point. It was not a matter of "receiving Jesus into their hearts" and then urging them to find a church (voluntary society) of their choice for fellowship. It was not a matter of an inner experience of justification or even of conversion that made them members of the spiritual or invisible body of Christ to be followed up by baptism and "joining church." It was not a matter of "saving their souls" and then gathering them into conventicles or visible religious societies.

Within the new group defined by allegiance to Jesus Christ they received the Holy Spirit, for it was the victorious Messiah and Lord of the new community who was giving the Spirit (v. 33). The Spirit of the ascended Christ now became the Spirit of his new body. Peter's promise that following repentance and baptism they would receive the gift of the Holy Spirit (v. 38) was not the promise of a "second experience" but the an-nouncement that it is within the community of the Spirit that the new reality is to be found. In later epi-sodes this connection between the Spirit and the Chris-tian community is also denoted by the gift of the Spirit coming as a result of apostolic laying on of hands (8:7; 19:6). The Spirit is the Spirit of the apostolic commu-nity — not, indeed, the possession of the apostles, as we learn in the Cornelius story (10:44-48), but the identi-fying hallmark and dynamic of the community.

Here, then, in the *koinonia* of the Spirit is the key to the gospel as announcement of present reality. The good news is of a saved and saving community which is constituted by the fruit of the Spirit — the "more excel-lent way" of love. It is not constituted by sacramental consecration, theological announcement, ecstatic expe-rience, or moralistic achievement. If such a reality of the Spirit does not exist, the gospel is of dubious signifi-cance for life in our contemporary secular existence.

CHAPTER TWO

The Apostolic Community

The Christian Church was born as a *mission to the world*. It was apostolic, i.e., sent into the world with a divine commission. That apostolic character is of its essence. If we may carry this imagery of birth further, we might say that the first cry of life from the newborn church was the proclamation that Jesus is the Lord of heaven and earth as well as the Messiah of the Jews (Acts 2:36).

The proclamation that Jesus is Lord and the formation of a new community had an inseparable organic relation to each other. Word and event together were proclamation of the new thing which God's Spirit was doing among men. What was proclaimed was the resurrection and victory of Jesus, the Messiah. What was historically demonstrated was a new community characterized by the Spirit of Jesus — the spirit of love and hope. Jesus' lordship was given form in the new resurrection community. Thus the reality of the new community was itself part of the proclamation. If the words about the historical Jesus or the ideal he portrayed are separated from a manifestation of the power and spirit of the living Christ in an actual community of redemption, they lack an adequate context of meaning.

The proclamation that Jesus is Lord both in word and event was directed outward to the world. His disciples were to be witnesses "to the end of the earth."

This outward directedness gave the new community the characteristics of a movement.[1] They announced that the "kingdom of God" had arrived and that it was destined to cover the earth and include all its people. They did not announce the formation of a new religious society gathered out of the larger social order to nourish and sustain itself as a community of faith. One joined the new movement in order to be part of God's mission to the world, not to escape from it or to set up some island of security in it. Thus the life of the first community was open to the world and by intention inclusive of it. What was done in the community was a sign and invitation to others to participate in the new reality which God had created by the Spirit of Christ.

The life and character of the new community were integral and essential to its witness. This point cannot be overemphasized today! The new spirit and practice of selfless sharing *(koinonia)* was central in the community life. This was the spirit (Spirit) of Jesus manifest in his followers. To be saved meant to participate in this new social reality created by the Spirit of Christ

---

1. Inasmuch as we will be using terms like movement, society, and sect frequently, it may be best to offer some definitions. A *society* is an organizationally defined association which forms on the basis of compatibility or agreed-upon regulations and goals. It is constituted by its organizational structure. While a society may be activity- or project-oriented and altruistic in its purposes, it exists for the members — for accomplishing their purposes and for whatever other advantages may come with membership.

A *club* has essentially the same character except that it generally is more oriented toward the self-fulfillment of the group.

A *sect* or *denomination* is a religious society in the above sense. The standards for membership are adherence to an agreed-upon religious faith and practice, and compatibility with the purposes of the organization. It seeks to perpetuate itself as an organized community through acquiring new members and thus to carry on its altruistic purposes.

A *movement* is less structured, more heterogeneous and flexible than a society. It is not organizationally defined. It gains its character and structure from the purpose for which it exists — its mission. But what is probably more significant is its relation to the whole (larger) group within which it operates. A movement aims to effect changes in the larger social order. It does not exist to perpetuate itself as a movement but to bring its purposes to realization within the whole social order of which it is a part.

and offered to the world. Even so, the apostles refused to accept responsibility for the organization and administration of this essential community function (Acts 6:2-4). This refusal has crucial significance for our understanding of the church and its mission.

The apostles have often been criticized for appointing deacons, or helpers, to administer relief and aid to the needy among them while they continued to concentrate on prayer and preaching. This is a case of misplaced spirituality, so the indictment runs. They did not see the holistic relation between the physical, social, and spiritual. They themselves failed to understand the profound significance of the new *koinoniac* reality which had emerged among them. On the other hand, modern evangelical commentators have lauded this as a precedent establishing the priority of the spiritual ministry of the word (preaching) in the mission of the church. Both of these arguments have missed the larger, central point implicit in their refusal.

The apostle bore in his calling and function the essential character of the new movement. The church is in essence the apostolic mission. Now an apostle is not in essence an administrator of a religious society, but a divinely commissioned messenger to lead a movement. That is why the apostles delegated this important but nevertheless secondary organizational responsibility to helpers. Had they accepted the role of administrators of internal affairs in the community, they would have subverted the integrity of the mission.

The complaint of the Hellenists was itself an implicit denial of the inclusive, open character of the new movement. They had already begun to think of the movement as a religious society or sect, and undoubtedly many of the converts likewise misunderstood. The significance of this story about internal difficulty (6:1-6) should be understood in light of the prior incident involving Ananias and Sapphira (5:1-11). The hypocrisy of Ananias and Sapphira threatened the integrity of the *koinonia* character of the mission. The Hellenists' complaint threatened the integrity of the mission of the *koinoniac* community. If the apostles had assumed the role of mutual aid administrators, they would have encouraged this misunderstanding. Within an apostolic context *koinonia* was itself part of the mission. Outside that apostolic context sharing becomes exclusive and sectarian.

The nature of the new community of the Spirit cannot be defined or understood apart from its being a witness to the lordship of Jesus Christ. In his book *The Nature and Mission of the Church,* Donald G. Miller quotes Emil Brunner as saying, "The church exists by mission as fire exists by burning!"[2] This is a happy metaphor in many ways.

The "Gospel of the Kingdom"

For over a century now Bible and prophetic conferences have rung the changes on the relation of the "kingdom" and the "church" in New Testament interpretation. This argument is important chiefly because it impinges directly on the practical matters of the mission and strategy of the church. What is the character of the church's mission in the world? How does it relate to the everyday "secular" life and social structure? What is the Holy Spirit's role in all of this? How does his presence relate to church activity on the one hand and secular activity on the other? What is the purpose and goal of the church's mission?

It is quite unnecessary for our discussion of these questions to enter into the more minuscule aspects of the long, ponderous, and sometimes tiresome debate about the order of events in God's plan for the consummation of history. In any case the more intricate blueprint of biblical prophecy will undoubtedly remain a moot issue. However, we do need to examine those larger aspects of the discussion which have a direct bearing upon the nature of the present mission and strategy of the apostolic community. Initially it was the deep concern of J. N. Darby and his associates about the condi-

2. Donald G. Miller, *The Nature and Mission of the Church,* John Knox, 1957, p. 69.

tion of Christendom and their convictions about the nature of the true church that gave rise to the dispensationalist theology. Much current evangelical terminology and debate about such issues as "postponement of the kingdom," "secret rapture," and the nature of the millennium hinge on the nature of the apostolic mission of the church.[3] Our concern in this chapter remains this initial and primary question — the nature of the church.

The discussion of New Testament interpretation has revolved around the question whether the kingdom of God/heaven has been "realized" in the resurrection of Christ and the formation of the church, or whether it has been postponed to a future fulfillment with the church as an interim arrangement.[4] How does the church relate to the ultimate goal of God in redeeming mankind and establishing his kingdom of righteousness?

It is well known that the phrase "kingdom of God," or "kingdom of heaven," is found very largely in the synoptic Gospels, where it is attributed to Jesus himself. Luke continues to use the phrase in Acts when he reports Paul's sermons, and there are scattered references in the Pauline letters and the general epistles, but the term is by no means so central in this part of the New Testament literature as in the synoptic Gospels. This rather striking shift in terminology along with other theological considerations has led a great many evangelical scholars to conclude that the church is something other than and quite distinct from the kingdom.

According to C. I. Scofield, whom many evangelical teachers follow, "rightly dividing the Word" means applying the epistles to the church age and most of the

3. See Kraus, *Dispensationalism in America: The Rise and Development,* John Knox, 1958; and Rowden, *The Origin of the Brethren 1825-1850,* Pickering and Inglis Ltd., 1967.

4. It is a happy omen when F. F. Bruce of Plymouth Brethren background writes in his commentary on *Acts* that he can adopt the words of C. H. Dodd with only "one qualification." He says, "Biblical eschatology is largely, but not completely, 'realized': there still remains a future element, to become actual at the Second Advent, the *parousia.* A balanced account of the NT presentation of the kingdom of God requires that due regard be paid to both of these aspects." See *The Book of Acts,* Eerdmans, 1954, pp. 35-36.

synoptic Gospels to the kingdom which Jesus offered to the Jews but postponed when they rejected him as their Messiah. According to this interpretation, the kingdom of God lies entirely in the future. It is a distinct era or "dispensation" in God's unfolding plan for history and will be fulfilled in the political dominion of Christ on earth in the millennium. The church's mission in the present dispensation is only indirectly related to the goals of the kingdom of God. Its mission is the salvation of individuals from a world that is doomed so that they may participate in the future kingdom.

Whether or not they subscribe to the finer points of dispensationalist eschatology, most Bible teachers and preachers in both the pietistic and pentecostal wings of evangelicalism do accept this theological view of church and kingdom, and model their congregational life and witness accordingly.

Both the centrality of Pentecost to the gospel, which we examined in the first chapter, and the continuity of the apostolic mission with that of Jesus himself raise questions about this view of a radical discontinuity between the church and kingdom. Those who first followed the risen Christ thought and spoke of themselves as a movement under a new ruler, i.e., "Lord and Messiah." When Peter on the day of Pentecost proclaimed Jesus to be "Lord and Messiah" and called men from the old nation or generation into the new one established by the Christ, he was obviously using kingdom terminology! Further, Luke represents Paul as preaching the "kingdom of God" in his ministry to the Gentiles, and Paul's use of the phrase in his epistles indicates that Luke has correctly represented him. Yet, it does seem obvious that the term is not so central for Paul as for Jesus. How then are we to account for the shift from "kingdom" to "church" terminology in the New Testament itself? And what does it imply about the apostles' self-understanding of their mission?

We shall postpone an elaboration of the meaning of the kingdom of God until the next chapter. Here the question is the relation of kingdom and church as it bears upon the mission and strategy of the church. (The order of discussion is dictated more by the historical circumstance of the debate than by logical order.) We must begin with some brief comments of definition.

The "kingdom of God" means God's saving, ruling presence. That rule has both a present and a future aspect. Where God is present in saving power, where his authority is acknowledged and his will is done on earth, there the presence of his kingdom is now manifest. Even now men and women enter that kingdom, and such children of the kingdom have "eternal life." The kingdom is among us as a kind of miraculous gift of God, but even as we acknowledge its presence we pray that it may come in its consummate fullness — "on earth as it is in heaven!" It is this dual nature of the kingdom as already present in power but not definable as a realm or political institution that raises the question of the church's relation to it. The church is not the kingdom. Yet it proclaims the "good news of the kingdom," and the "keys of the kingdom" have been entrusted to it.

The typical evangelical Protestant solution is to relegate the kingdom to the realm of "spiritual" and individual experience. For example, George Eldon Ladd, who has greatly illuminated many aspects of the discussion in his *The Gospel of the Kingdom,* explains the "mystery of the kingdom" as follows:

> What Jesus meant is this. "Yes, the Kingdom of God is here. But there is a mystery — a new revelation about the Kingdom. The Kingdom of God is here; but instead of destroying human sovereignty, it has attacked the sovereignty of Satan. The Kingdom of God is here; but instead of making changes in the external, political order of things, it is making changes in the spiritual order and in the lives of men and women."[5]

This solution does not do justice to the New Testament view of the centrality of the church of God in his plan for the salvation of the world. Karl Schmidt observes in his article on "*Basileus* and Its Correlates in the New Testament" that in the case of Jesus and his

---

5. *The Gospel of the Kingdom,* Eerdmans, 1971, p. 55.

apostles "it is not the individual as such who receives the promises, but only the congregation, as a member of which the individual receives salvation."[6]

The New Testament word for church or congregation is *ekklesia*, which means literally "assembly." The word is often used to indicate the assemblies or centers of God's kingdom after the analogy of the imperial colonies throughout the Roman empire — e.g., the assemblies at Thessalonica, Philippi, and Corinth. It is also used in the singular to indicate the unity of the movement under its one Lord — the church throughout the world; however, this latter usage is far less common than the first.

Paul specifically used the metaphor of the Roman colony to describe the Christian center at Philippi (Phil. 3:20). The city itself was such a colony or military outpost of the Roman government. Just so, the congregation was an outpost of God's kingdom ruled from heaven. From Paul's letter we learn that this small outpost had been withstanding heavy attack for their aggressive promotion of the gospel. Indeed, Paul himself is writing from jail, where he is under indictment for subversion of the Roman government. Nevertheless, his main concern is the advance of the cause. He urges party unity and team spirit as they strive shoulder to shoulder for the gospel faith. The political imagery is obvious. This is kingdom talk!

The concept of God's kingdom is also implicit in the many references to Jesus as Lord and head of the church. Already in the teaching of Jesus, his presence and message are virtually equated with the presence of the kingdom of God. In Luke 11:20 and its parallels, for example, Jesus' ministry of exorcism is proclaimed as an immediate manifestation of the kingdom. The Palm Sunday crowds hailed the entry of Jesus into

---

6. *Theological Dictionary of the New Testament*, edited by Gerhard Kittel, Vol. I, Eerdmans, 1964, p. 586. It is clear that much of what Ladd says in his study of the kingdom of God leads to this same conclusion, but he himself does not elaborate the implications of this. The best single study of these implications is to be found in John Howard Yoder's *The Politics of Jesus*, Eerdmans, 1972.

Jerusalem as the entry of "the king who comes in the name of the Lord," and as the coming of the kingdom of David (Mark 11:10). Again in Luke 18:29 and parallels, Jesus' "name," the "gospel," and the "kingdom of God" are used synonymously. This kind of easy parallelism suggests that the church associated in the closest way the presence of the Spirit of Christ and the presence of the kingdom of God. Its recognition that the redeeming rule of God had broken uniquely into history in Jesus Christ was proclaimed in its confession that Jesus is Lord. In the closing paragraph of his more detailed review of this kind of New Testament data, Schmidt concludes: "It is not the case that the emphasis on the Church has supplanted Jesus of Nazareth's preaching of the Kingdom of God. Rather it is the case that in the post-Easter experience of Christ the belief in the Kingdom of God remained firm."[7]

The use of new terminology can be accounted for most simply by the observation that "kingdom of God" is a colloquial Jewish expression that needed translation in the Gentile setting. *Ekklesia* was an indigenous Hellenistic term with political overtones that made it acceptable as a translation of terms like "people," "synagogue," or "kingdom of God." It did not in the first instance have the connotation of a religious society. Further, *ekklesia* was a far more concrete word to use in referring to the multiplying centers throughout the Roman empire. It seems quite unnecessary, therefore, to elaborate a complex theory of discontinuity between church and kingdom which involves God in a major strategy change to account for this shift in terminology. Furthermore, such a theory willy-nilly makes the church peripheral to God's plan of salvation in a way that is quite foreign to the New Testament.

To be sure there were changes in the life of the church as Christianity became predominantly a Gentile movement. For example, the conceptualization of Christ and his relation to the churches was modified with

---

7. *Op. cit.,* p. 589.

the passing of time and the change of cultural context. One would hardly expect Jewish associations of a political Messiah to cling to the term. A shift in emphasis from proclamation *(kerygma)* to moral teaching *(didache)* also seems to have occurred, as relatively more elementary explanation was required for the new recruits. Then too, the apostles seem to have become progressively aware that their mission would not be triumphantly consummated in the immediate future. (They apparently clung for a while to the hope of an immediate restoration of political authority to Israel in spite of Jesus' disclaimer!) Such changes, however, do not necessarily indicate a radical change in the apostolic self-understanding of the church's nature and mission.

Without pressing further the details of argumentation, let me offer several New Testament affirmations which have a direct bearing on the mission and nature of the apostolic movement. First, the New Testament clearly speaks of a future revelation *(epiphania)* at the end of this era which is both *climax* to what has preceded and *inauguration* of a new era. In this respect the second advent parallels the first. Note that two things are said in this affirmation. To speak of the end as climax or consummation is to relate it to the historical chain of events which precede it. It does not come as a tour de force — an arbitrary act of power cancelling what has preceded. It will be a *fulfillment*. The further manifestation will be simply a fuller disclosure of "this same Jesus" (Acts 1:11). That is why the future presence *(parousia)* must be called the *second* advent.

But while it is climactic, it is also the initiation of that which is new and different. This final manifestation presents us with more than the accumulative effects of the activity of the "church militant." It will be a new, decisive manifestation of Christ's lordship as "King of kings, and Lord of lords." It was the weakness of the classical Augustinian model, sometimes called post-millennialism, especially in its liberal, evolutionary form, that it did not adequately recognize this new aspect of the second advent.

Finally, a significant advance in God's plan for history has been inaugurated by Jesus in his first advent. The commission for carrying out this phase of the operation has been given to the apostolic community — the church. To use a parallel from Israel's history, the Jordan has been crossed, the troops assigned, and the conquest of Canaan begun.

This is the central message of *Ephesians,* which unfolds the "mystery" of God's plan for history. Paul first states that the disclosure was made "in Christ" (1:9). It is Christ who has broken down the old ethnic and religious barriers between Jewish Israel and the nations (2:14). He is the "chief cornerstone" in the new structure being built as a "dwelling place of God in the Spirit" (2:19-22). The content of the mystery which Paul unfolded turns out to be precisely the message of Pentecost, namely, that membership in the community of the Spirit has been extended universally through the good news. The nations are being offered a share in the fulfillment of "the promise in Christ Jesus through the gospel" (3:1-6). And further, this new phase which is elsewhere referred to as "the rule of God" is being demonstrated (made known) to the cosmic powers and authorities *through the church* (3:7-13).

Both Paul and Luke give a central place to the church, i.e., the apostolic mission, as the spearhead of the kingdom. Lampe has pointed out that of all the Gospels it is Luke who emphasizes the significance of the church in the further advance of the kingdom of God. He notes the explicit parallels between Jesus' messianic mission through the power of the Spirit and the continuation of that same mission by his chosen disciples who receive a baptism of the Spirit for mission.[8] This does not mean that the disciples, as agents of the Holy Spirit, bring in the kingdom. It does, however, indicate that the work of the disciples is kingdom work.

Paul, as we have noted, makes the same point in the Ephesian epistle. The church is in the center of God's

---

8. *Studies in the Gospels,* especially pp. 168, 194.

plan for advancing the gospel of the kingdom. Paul presents himself as the commissioned representative of the "Lord" and the apostolic community. He is Christ's ambassador to the Gentiles, offering them a place in the new reality which God is creating. And he calls them to become part of the church — the "new man," the "new commonwealth," the "household of God" — which has been commissioned to make known or demonstrate the "gospel of peace" to the fragmented, hostile powers of this age.

There is only one gospel. The gospel of the kingdom is the gospel of Christ. Christ is both the message and the messenger. As message he is the one in whom the presence and power of God unto salvation becomes reality. As messenger he proclaims the rule or kingdom of God — that in a decisive, new way God's presence and power are manifest among us. The gospel of Christ is the gospel of the kingdom, and the apostolic community has been commissioned to advance this good news with all its attending implications.[9]

Movement or Society?

For the layman, New Testament language in the standard translations has almost become jargon, filled with specialized terms not denoting familiar, everyday meanings. This unfortunate circumstance is the reason for the multitude of translations which have flooded the market in recent years. What, for example, does the term "kingdom of heaven" convey to most contemporary Christians? By and large those whom I have questioned simply take it as a synonym of heaven. This has led to much ambiguity and misunderstanding of the issues. All of us are familiar with the almost universal Sunday School question whether a rich person can go to heaven when he dies. But Jesus was not speaking primarily of a rich person's future destiny. It was the rich person's

---

9. Claude Welch writes: "The church is always 'for a purpose,' and the final end of its being is always God and his Kingdom" (*The Reality of the Church*, p. 211).

availability now as a follower and disciple that concerned Jesus.

In the early 1960's Clarence Jordan, who was making a colloquial paraphrase of the New Testament, was searching for a term to translate the phrase "kingdom of God." What modern term would convey the implications and feelings which that phrase stirred up in the mind of a first-century Jew? Being very much aware of the newly emerging civil rights movement in the Black churches of the South, he hit upon the happy phrase "the God Movement." Thus according to Jordan's translation Jesus came preaching that the God Movement was about to begin.[10]

Put in these terms we can begin to see in a new light the issues at stake in the argument about the relation of the kingdom of heaven and the church. The question now becomes whether the church is a vital part of the God Movement. Is the church another religious society or club which provides its members the special privileges of club membership? Is it an interim missionary society organized for recruiting new members while we wait for the reintroduction of the God Movement at some auspicious moment in the future? Or is it an integral functioning part of a movement successfully begun by the Christ who now directs it by his Spirit? Today it almost seems incredible that anyone would ever have equated the church with the God Movement, as some Christians in a more optimistic age did. But is it not a vital part of it?

Perhaps this is the place to pause and look further at the significance of describing the church as a movement rather than a religious society. The word movement suggests dynamic and action. A movement forms as a consequence of powerful convictions or events which call for action and change in response. Mission rather than organizational structure gives cohesiveness and form to a movement. Organization is secondary and is

10. See Clarence Jordan, *The Cotton Patch Version of Matthew and John,* Association Press, 1970.

determined by the nature of the mission which actually constitutes the movement.

An even more fundamental characteristic of a movement is its dynamic and open relationship to the larger social order within which it operates. A movement seeks to effect change in that social order. It tries to turn the direction of historical development. Thus it does not understand itself as a separate or peripheral subculture but as a dynamic for change within the dominant culture.[11] According to the New Testament, this is the nature of the God Movement. It does not have organizationally defined boundaries. Jesus likened it to yeast in dough, to salt in food, to light shining in the dark, and to a seed that grows into a tree.

It is this dynamic movement of God in and for the world that provides the context for all the life and work of the church whether it be evangelism, education, mutual aid, or social service. Let us look more carefully at the implications of this way of viewing the church.

In the first place, when the church is defined as movement, the requirement for membership will be agreement with and commitment to the goals and methods of the God Movement. The criterion for belonging is commitment to the Christ as leader of the movement. The password is "Christ is Lord." This commitment is more important than agreement with correct theological formulas, a qualifying religious experience, or assent to a particular moral discipline. Loyalty, trust, and serious involvement are of the essence in a movement.

In the second place, this movement context for the life of the church directly implies that whatever the church does as a social organization should effectively contribute to the central purpose of the God Movement. Nothing must get in the way of that. The church does many things. It educates, but it is not primarily an

11. Obviously the way in which a movement operates in its environing social order is historically conditioned. Sometimes it must exist underground (the early church). Sometimes it may function openly as part of a democratic process (Western Christianity today). The important thing is that it should not misunderstand its mission!

educational institution. Neither should it educate indiscriminately. It does social service, but it is not a social service agency. Its service programs should be strictly in line with the mission of God in the world.[12] It propagandizes and evangelizes, but not in order to build itself as a powerful and prestigious institution. It provides for corporate worship, but it is not a society for the cultivation of congregational liturgy or private meditation. It shares its goods with the needy in brotherly concern, but it is neither a mutual insurance company nor a relief organization. All of these things are good in themselves, but they may or may not be strategic to the apostolic mission. That mission and the immediate circumstances in which it must be carried out must be allowed to determine priorities and the shape of the various programs.

In the third place, the church is that community in which the purposes and ideals of the movement become a reality in the life and history of the secular order. The church is the secular — i.e., temporal or historical — expression of the Movement. It is a demonstration of the new reconciled order of society under the rule of God. Such an expression or demonstration of the new reality is part of the church's strategy for proclaiming the rule of God to the larger social order.

Within its ordered life the church should demonstrate the spirit of God in a community of justice, mutuality, respect, and forgiveness which are the signs of *agape*. In short it should reflect the qualities of brotherhood or *koinonia* which it proclaims. Like a city on a hill it should be an example or light to the world in its own organized life. It is the reconciled community which by its very life bears witness to the movement of God among men.

Throughout history this has been the ideal of the monastic orders, sectarian groups such as the Mennonites and the Holiness churches, and many other religious communal groups. They have viewed the church as a spiritual community separated from the world but dem-

---

12. I have elaborated this point in *The Healing Christ*, Herald, 1972.

onstrating to it the new life of holy living, loving concern, and mutual support among their own members. This is an important aspect of the witness which has largely been lost in contemporary urban Protestant churches. Unfortunately, it is all too easy for such "separation" to become withdrawal from the world with the accompanying loss of active concern for it.

The church also must exist *in the world* to which it has been sent as a minister of reconciliation. This aspect of its life and work has sometimes been called its secular mission.[13] The church exists as the secular community of the Spirit in the sense that it is a social institution alongside other social institutions. It is a historically and culturally conditioned expression of the God Movement. Thus it must inevitably interact with the secular communities of business, industry, labor, government, and other social institutions. It cannot — indeed must not try to — evade the issues raised by class distinctions, discrimination, poverty, secular ideologies, revolutionary political movements, national and sectional rivalries, and the like.

In this role the church operates in terms of the Movement's purposes and goal as a "colony of heaven" and may often be in tension and even open conflict with purely secular loyalties, methods, and goals. Unfortunately the church in history has too often compromised its own essential nature as an expression and base of operation for the God Movement by attempting to remain aloof from secular involvement or even by overtly supporting a demonic status quo.

Examples of the points at which the church as a secular community of the Spirit intersects with the world can be drawn from either the New Testament or from the twentieth-century situation. Passages from Paul like Galatians 3:27-28, Colossians 3:10-11, Philemon, I

---

13. Secular, as I have indicated, means first of all temporal or historical. My point here is made if we contrast religious or sacred to secular. The church must see itself as a part of the "everyday," "this-worldly" life of man. This was the main thrust of Colin Williams' two essays, *What in the World?* (National Council of Churches, 1964) and *Where in the World?* (NCC, 1963).

Corinthians 7:29-31, and Romans 13 recognize the issues in the first-century situation. Today the problems of racial discrimination, economic and political injustice, poverty and growing inequality, class distinctions, war and nationalism, and ideological tensions still confront the church.

The apostolic mission of the church as the secular community of the Spirit requires that it confront and challenge unrighteousness simply by the fact of its existence in the world as a new creation where the old hostilities, discriminations, and loyalties are no longer recognized because the peace of God already reigns in its midst. To capitulate to the pressures and blandishments of secular society is to deny the Lord of the Movement. To accept a position of neutrality and uninvolvement is to contradict the very essence of the evangelical mission.

If the organized church in the United States had demonstrated the new reality of social and racial equality before God in its own life as part of secular society, it could have prevented from the beginning much of the degradation and misery caused by segregation.[14] If the churches in Russia, Cuba, and Spain, for example, had taken seriously their responsibility for economic justice, might not the bloodshed of violent revolutions have been averted? If the billions of dollars of church money which are invested in ways that undergird and augment the old order of injustice were reinvested in Movement causes, what miracles of grace might the church be empowered to do! It is not a matter of advising the government or other institutions of the world order, although at times that may be called for. Rather Christians should assume their responsibility to demonstrate the "new creation" that has come to birth as a historical reality in the life and mission of the God Movement.

---

14. In *The Racial Problem in Christian Perspective* (Harper & Row, 1959), Kyle Haselden points out that the signs "White" and "Colored" were posted in the churches before they were posted in public facilities. In the beginning of the Pentecostal movement in the United States, the gospel overcame segregation, but in the period 1914-1925 the churches capitulated to the segregation laws that forbade Christians to worship together.

In the fourth place, the church should be a kind of propaganda ministry for the God Movement. The good news of God's redeeming activity has been disclosed to the church, and to it has been given the commission to bear witness and make disciples of all nations. Out of the reality of its own new life in Christ the church seeks to bring the rule of God into reality both in the life of individuals and in society at large. To men individually the church proclaims the good news of God's redemptive activity in and through Jesus Christ, and it calls them to respond in commitment to his leadership by identifying with the Movement. To those who embody institutional power and authority — "the powers that be" — it announces the fact of God's rule and calls them to fulfill their respective roles in human society in submission to his authority and plan.[15]

The church does not claim to be expert in diplomacy, legislation, or social engineering. But it does claim to know a good deal about the divine intention for human society. It therefore rebukes dishonesty, injustice, violence, and selfishness in the public administration of the social order, and it calls men and institutions to follow the way of righteousness, love, and peace.

In summary, the church should be seen as part of the God Movement. It has been given the mission to spread the good news that the "rule of God is at hand," and to call men to change their ways and live in light of the new reality. Of course the church has a life of its own which must be nurtured and nourished, but it is not *for* itself. Its life is, like its Master's, given for the world.[16] It shares in his sufferings in order that it might

---

15. The Anabaptists, who reintroduced the believers' church in the Reformation, were ardent evangelists calling men into the true church. They were deeply conscious, however, that the activity of God was not limited to the church and that his rule extends over all men whether they recognize Christ or not. Therefore, while not confusing the role of church and government, they did not hesitate to confront magistrates with the biblical requirements for their office. Menno Simons is a good example of this.

16. See Langdon Gilkey, *How the Church Can Minister to the World Without Losing Itself*, Harper & Row, 1964, especially chapter 3, for an excellent discussion. He writes, "Some form of the social

share in his triumph. It must lose its life for his sake and the gospel's in order to find it. Its very essence is apostolic mission.

---

gospel is a requirement for a holy church in the world, lest it capitulate entirely to the world and lose its own being" (p. 71).

CHAPTER THREE

The Saving Community

From the earliest centuries of the Christian movement the church has been compared to the ark of Noah outside of which there was no salvation from the flood. The actual phrase *extra ecclesiam nulla salus* (outside the church no salvation) is attributed to Cyprian, bishop of Carthage about 250 A.D., but the kernel of the idea is obviously found already in the New Testament. As we have seen, Peter identified salvation with entrance into the new Messianic community in his sermon at Pentecost. Paul virtually equated "baptism into Christ" and "baptism into the body of Christ." In Ephesians Paul speaks of pagans as under God's wrath "alienated from the commonwealth of Israel," and he describes the salvation accomplished "in the blood of Christ" as peace and reconciliation to God "in one body through the cross." Salvation for the Gentiles means citizenship with the saints and membership in the "household of God" (Eph. 2:11-19).

When salvation progressively came to be equated with the gift of immortal life and freedom from the penalty of sin, the church perceived itself as the *agent* of that salvation. Through the mystery of the sacraments consecrated by the catholic or orthodox clergy, guilt of sin could be assuaged and escape from deserved penalty assured. Salvation was attached to the cult of a divine institution, and *extra ecclesiam nulla salus* coalesced with the claim that the apostolic church held the keys to heaven! This is a far cry from the New Testament conviction that new life in Christ is to be found in the community of the Spirit.

The Protestant reformers of the sixteenth century were quite correct in rejecting the institutional perversion of the medieval papacy, but unfortunately they sought to correct the error by spiritualizing the "true" church which is the community of salvation. For Luther the true church is "hidden," and for Calvin it is "invisible." It emerges for Luther in the universal communion of saints where the activities of spiritual life are observable, but it is not embodied in a living congregation of saints. For Calvin the true church is the body of the elect known only to God, and although it subsists as a body of inward faith in the local congregation, it is invisible to human discernment.

This concept of the church corresponds to a concept of salvation which was likewise spiritualized. Salvation was by theological definition a purely supernatural act and therefore nothing which could be clearly identified with the attitude or action of any human individual or group. It was understood as an inward theological transaction (justification) which could not be directly correlated with ethical behavior and human relationships. Its most obvious indicator was faith, but faith is an inward attitude which again cannot be more than presumptively equated with a confession or intellectual assent to orthodox Christian doctrine. Thus salvation could only be described as a private transaction strictly between the individual person and God. It was to be hoped that visible manifestations (works) would follow, but as defined in Protestant orthodoxy they were not of the essence.

With such working definitions it was virtually impossible to recapture the social dynamic of biblical salvation. Rather than an experience of God's renewal and life together in a visible community of God's people, salvation was construed as a private transaction largely restricted to the intellect (correct thinking) and to the religious or spiritual aspects of life. Since the "spiritual" is an essentially private category and known only to God, life together in the Christian congregation was lived under the rubric of orthodox doctrine and sacrament (Lutheran) with the addition of prescribed discipline in strict Calvinistic parishes.

Happily, as we have seen, not all life in the seventeenth-century parish moved at this minimal level, but this was the theological rationale under which the Protestant congregation operated. As a result the integral organic relation between salvation and life in the visible body of Christ was unwittingly severed. At its best this way of viewing the relation of the church and salvation portrays the church as a spiritual network of elect individuals who have a "new position in Christ," and live in a vital "mystical union" with him, but who cannot be identified with any visible organized group of believers.[1] The visible church is simply a voluntary association of individuals making a religious profession. Some of these members have been "saved" quite independently and apart from their membership in the visible congregation. Many others are "carnal" or hypocritical professors.

During the time of the Reformation a third alternative to Roman Catholicism and classical Protestantism was offered by the evangelical Anabaptists; but under the heavy hand of persecution and oppression it was smothered. That alternative suggested that "salvation by grace through faith" should be understood in terms of new birth, conversion, and life in the visible body of

---

1. See L. S. Chafer, *Systematic Theology*, Vol. VII, Dallas Seminary, 1948, pp. 127f. John Calvin gives relatively more significance to membership in the visible church. He discusses the church under the heading of "External Means of Grace." The visible church is for the "motherly care" and "nourishment" of those who by a "secret election and inner call" belong to the true, invisible church. "But because a small and contemptible number are hidden in a huge multitude and a few grains of wheat are covered by a pile of chaff, we must leave to God alone the knowledge of his church, whose foundation is his secret election" (*Institutes of the Christian Religion*, IV, 1,2. See LIBRARY OF CHRISTIAN CLASSICS, Vol. 22, p. 1013).

Christ. The concepts of justification and forgiveness were also affirmed, but they were not equated with salvation. If Luther's characteristic emphasis can be captured in the phrase "the just shall live *by* faith," Menno Simons' emphasis was that "the just shall live his faith."[2] In a particularly beautiful passage he wrote:

> For he who is a Christian must follow the Spirit, Word, and example of Christ, no matter whether he be emperor, king, or whatever he be. For these following admonitions apply to all alike: Let this mind be in you which was also in Christ Jesus. Phil. 2:5. He that saith he abideth in him, ought himself also so to walk, even as he walked. I John 2:6.[3]

Salvation by grace was understood as a living relationship and walk in the true visible church of Christ. Indeed, for Menno the marks of the true visible congregation included love for the brother concretely expressed in the life of the community.[4]

Today two seemingly contrary phenomena are juxtaposed on the American religious scene. On the one hand sagging church roles and a sense of what Elton Trueblood has called "futility" in the pew indicate a great uneasiness about the viability of organized religion. On the other hand there is an unprecedented search for mystical experience and religious reality in mass revivals as well as in lonely submission to a guru. Perhaps the renewed emphasis upon religious conventicles, *koinonia* groups, communal colonies, house churches, prayer cells, and awareness groups represents an emerging synthesis in this dialectic of individual experience and organized religion.

At any rate we seem to have come to a crucial juncture in the life of the American churches. The latent human-

---

2. *The Complete Writings of Menno Simons*, Herald, 1956, p. 369. Menno wrote: "For if we had the spirit, faith, and power of Zacchaeus, which we verily should have,...there would soon be a different and better situation because, it cannot fail, *the righteous must live his faith*." See also his discussion of justification in his pamphlet entitled "Distressed Christians" on pages 503-08. This is one of his best.

3. *Ibid.*, p. 922.

4. *Ibid.*, pp. 739-43. See also Franklin Littell, *A Tribute to Menno*, Herald, 1961, pp. 23-36.

ism of liberal Protestantism and the spiritualizing of fundamentalist Protestantism have both foundered on the same shoal, namely, individualism. Liberalism championed the rational, liberated individual who joined with others of his own persuasion to build the "democracy of God," as George Coe called it. Fundamentalism championed the supernaturally "born again" individual who was vitally joined to the spiritual body but only incidentally to a particular congregation for nurture and worship. Neither viewed life in community as integral to the salvation of the individual. Perhaps the inchoate alternative offered by the sixteenth-century Anabaptists can give us a new lead and model for understanding the meaning of salvation in community today.

Salvation by Christ

The New Testament writers are quite definite and explicit about the meaning of salvation and its intrinsic relation to Jesus of Nazareth. Salvation was a common pursuit in the ancient world. Many itinerant "evangelists" peddled their schemes of salvation and offered their "miraculous" evidences. Thus it was important for the apostles to differentiate the salvation offered by Jesus Christ from that of the Simon Maguses who roamed the ancient world.

The hallmark of the salvation which the apostles proclaimed was the Savior himself. Jesus Christ was called the "author and perfecter" of the new way (Heb. 12:2). He was the "pioneer" or original source of salvation (Heb. 2:10). The Christian faith took both its origin and its character from him. He is called redeemer, "Author of life," sacrificial lamb, priestly mediator, prophet of God, and anointed King. Indeed, the name Jesus means "Jahweh saves," and the apostles made the forthright claim that "there is salvation in no one else, for there is no other name under heaven given among men by which we must be saved" (Acts 4:12). In the same vein Paul wrote to the Corinthian church, "I was determined to know nothing among you but Christ crucified" (I Cor. 2:2).

The salvation of which Jesus was "pioneer and per-fecter" is described in a rich variety of metaphors drawn from everyday life in the ancient world. There are the ritual metaphors of washing, sacrifice, and consecration. There are figures associated with freedom — redemption from bondage to an alien law and ransom from slavery to sin and Satan. There are the references· to salvation as new life — new birth, resurrection, new creation, and regeneration. Salvation is changing one's whole way of thinking and turning in a new direction — repentance and conversion. It is a renewal and reorientation of life. It means release from the guilt of sin and reconciliation with God and man — forgiveness, justification, and "peace with God through our Lord, Jesus Christ." None of these may be used exclusively to present a theology of salvation. Rather they are like the facets of a superb and finely polished diamond which reflect back the brilliance of God's revelation in Christ.

All of these descriptions find their place and signifi-cance under the dominant motif of the new covenant and community of salvation which Jesus inaugurated. As we have noted in the earlier chapters, at least by implication, the work of Jesus as Messiah was twofold. First, he presented and ratified a new covenant agree-ment from God. Second, under the terms of the newly established agreement he formed the new *koinonia* or *ekklesia* of the Spirit. The first was accomplished in his life and death as the "lamb of God" and is symbolized in the broken bread and cup of wine which he shared with his disciples at the Last Supper. "This cup," he said, "is the new covenant in my blood" (I Cor. 11:25). The second and consummating aspect of his messianic task was realized in the new outpouring of the Spirit and the creation of the *koinonia* of salvation — the new people of God.

Luke presents what Jesus "began to do and teach" in his Gospel narrative. According to his account Jesus came preaching the "good news of the kingdom of God" in the cities of Judea (4:42), but when he was rejected by the leaders and misunderstood by the multitudes, "he chose twelve from among his disciples whom he named apostles" (6:12-16). This was the beginning of the new community which he was forming. After he had chosen the representatives of the new Israel, he presented to them the terms of the new covenant in the "Sermon on the Plain" (6:20-49). To these twelve men he disclosed his true nature and mission as they lived together in a community of teacher and disciples. Then, after a period of training and discipline, he sealed the new covenant "in his blood" and left them with the promise that he would drink the symbolic cup anew with them in the kingdom of God. The literary parallelism with the Exodus account and the formation of Israel into a covenant people is unmistakable.

There can be no doubt that this "Savior" understood his essential task to be the formation of a new covenant community. Having been rejected by the "old crooked generation" (Acts 2:40), he exercised his messianic prerogative to initiate the new *ekklesia* (Mt. 16:18-19). As George Ladd points out, *ekklesia* (church)

> is the word most commonly used in the Greek Old Testament to refer to Israel as the people of God. The very use of this word suggests that our Lord purposed to bring into existence a new people who would take the place of the old Israel who rejected both His claim to Messiahship and His offer of the Kingdom of God.[5]

To this new community Jesus entrusted the "kingdom of God," which was, he said, taken away from national Israel who had been unfaithful (Mt. 21:43; see also 8:12; 11:11-20). From now on the forward thrust of God's plan for the redemption of mankind under his

---

5. George Eldon Ladd, *The Gospel of the Kingdom*, Eerdmans, 1971, p. 112. In the following discussion Ladd notes, "No longer is the Kingdom of God active in the world through Israel; it works rather through the church." See his discussion on pages 113ff.

The kingdom of God is synonymous with the Old Testament phrase "the salvation of Jahweh." It is the end of alienation and rebellion against his will as we pray in the Lord's Prayer. From Matthew's use of the phrase in 19:16-30, it is synonymous with being saved and inheriting eternal life. Note how this language is used interchangeably.

rule would find its channel and focus in the new community of the Spirit (Eph. 1:9ff.; 3:10-12).

In this setting we can interpret the significance and meaning of Jesus' word to Peter about the keys of the kingdom (Mt. 16:18). Peter represented the *ekklesia* in formation, and to him are given the keys of the kingdom. He and his fellow disciples were entrusted with the authority to "bind and loose" — i.e., to open and close the gates to the kingdom of God (Mt. 18:18-20; John 20:22-23). Matthew 16:19 seems to refer most immediately to opening the secret of Jesus' identity as the messianic Savior. This authority to open the kingdom is re-delegated by the risen Christ, who commissioned the eleven to "go into all the world and make disciples" (Mt. 28:19). Luke also at least indirectly refers to it when he notes that the first congregation at Jerusalem "devoted themselves to the *apostles' teaching*."[6]

The wording of Matthew 18 and John 20 suggests a different aspect of the church's authority and responsibility. In these passages the binding and loosing relate directly to maintaining the integrity of the new covenant fellowship under the rule of God. Here the "binding and loosing" does not connote a legal or sacramental authority to grant absolution from mortal sin. Rather it is a matter of the reality and quality of *koinonia* in the saving community. This is explicit in the Matthew 18 context, where the problem referred to is brotherly offense. The threat of hypocrisy and selfishness received the most severe rebukes in the newly formed Christian movement because such attitudes pervert the reality of a saving community. Peter called the hypocrisy of Ananias a falsification of the Holy Spirit which is the spirit of the new community (Acts 5:3).

The disciple band which received the Holy Spirit (John 20) and within whose midst the Christ is present (Mt. 18) opens the possibility of salvation in the kingdom of God. It is the community where Christ's peace reigns; where *koinonia* is realized; where the Spirit is

---

6. See Marlin Jeschke, *Discipling the Brother*, Herald, 1972; especially chapter 2, pp. 41-56.

poured out; and where persons are released from their sins. The inauguration of this saving reality at Pentecost and its surprising, exciting emergence in the life of the apostolic movement is so obvious that it needs little comment. What is needed today is a fresh sense of that same saving reality.

Salvation from Sin

We live in a culture and society that is dominated by what B. F. Skinner calls "aversive reinforcement," or punishment.[7] We depend to a far larger extent on punitive measures to control deviant behavior than on an appeal to the well-being of individuals and society. We spank our children, jail our criminals, bomb our enemies, and in many less overt ways even manipulate our friends into the kind of behavior we wish through the threat of nonacceptance. Motivation stemming from feelings of guilt and fear of punishment plays a large role in our behavioral patterns.

This is and has been true also in the domain of religion. Much evangelical preaching has tried to induce conviction by preaching law and judgment. Implicit in the definition of grace have been overtones of the recipient's worthlessness and guilt. Grace has been construed as giving what is not deserved to the unworthy. Justice, that magnificent word of the Hebrew prophets denoting a condition of equity and righteousness among God's people, has been reduced in meaning to Aristotle's punitive justice. Consequently grace has been defined largely as mercy, the reprieve of just and deserved penalty. Salvation is understood as rescue from punishment —forgiveness and escape from the legal consequences of sin.

No one who has known the forgiveness and acceptance of Christian love will wish to downgrade the quality of mercy in God's grace. But one must protest the unwholesome reductionism in the emphasis upon salvation as reprieve from the punitive consequences of sin and

---

7. See B. F. Skinner, *Beyond Freedom and Dignity*, Knopf, 1971; especially chapters 2 and 4.

the interpretation of grace simply as mercy. This con-
striction of meaning begins with the interpretation of
covenant law within the political category of legal statutes and classifying sin under the category of crime.
Thus, as we noted, grace has been interpreted as par-
doning mercy in contrast to justice, which requires an
equivalent penalty. While the human legal system is
indeed one metaphor to describe the nature of God's
covenant with man and his transgression against that
covenant, it by no means provides us a full-orbed view
of biblical salvation.

In Scripture salvation is deliverance from sin itself
and not merely from the legal consequences of transgression. Grace comes first as the word of God the
Creator affirming the goodness of his creation. It comes
second as the word of the Creator-Redeemer continuing
his affirmation of creation's essential goodness in the face
of existential failure and error. It is the affirmation of
worth in the imperfect and the creative acceptance of
our second best which enables us to become what the
Creator originally intended us to be! Grace is God's
goodness and beauty reproducing itself in human frailty.

Law, or Torah, does not mean primarily legal statutes
which are enforced by punitive sanctions. It is first of all
the "covenant of life and peace" (Mal. 2:5) between
God and his people. It is a recognition of the order and
purpose inherent in creation. It is the way of the Lord
with his people (Ps. 119). Indeed, so essential is God's
law to human well-being that both in the ancient
Hebrew and in the early Christian communities law
was understood as one of the gracious gifts of God to
man. Disobedience of such a law is simultaneously self-
destructive (death) and God-denying (rebellion).

Seen in this context, sin cannot be understood simply
as an act of transgression to which extrinsic penal consequences are assigned. In other words, it cannot be cata-
logued and dealt with as a crime against law. Sin and
its consequences are so integrally related that they must
be viewed as a condition in which the human family
lives and from which it needs redemption. Salvation is

deliverance from sin. It is described as the reign of peace *(shalom)* and justice—"the righteousness of God" which we are to seek above all else. Salvation means the restoration of a covenant relationship between man and God, and man and his fellowmen.

In his letter to the Ephesians, Paul characterizes sin as alienation from the covenant community. The plight of the unsaved Gentiles is not portrayed as wickedness and individual moral debauchery for which they need an atoning sacrifice of equivalent moral or legal severity. Rather Paul wrote that they were "separated from Christ, alienated from the commonwealth of Israel, and strangers to the covenants of promise." Because of this they were "without hope and without God in the world." Their worldly allegiance had been to the "prince of the power of the air." They were motivated by the "spirit which is at work in the sons of disobedience." Under this allegiance and power they walked in trespasses and sins—"in the course of this world." In like manner he describes their salvation in terms of reconciliation and participation in the covenant community established in the "blood of Christ."

Sin means broken relationship. It is a rejection of God's goodness, and at the same time a refusal to love. Its most obvious manifestations are the selfish competition, fearful struggle for survival, and prideful discrimination which destroy the possibility of personal fulfillment in a community of love. Salvation is the restoration of relationship in covenant community.

Salvation as Restoration of Community

There is among us today a new awareness of salvation as the restoration of wholeness to man. There is new appreciation for the interrelation of body and spirit in the unity of personhood. The word "psychosomatic" has become common parlance, and lip service at least is paid to the idea that salvation includes the "whole man." This is good, but we need to go a step further and recognize that the whole person is person-in-community. The autonomous individual is not a whole person. The autonomous person is not a saved person. The religious ideal of Christianity is not the ascetic mystic who has cut himself off from others in order to achieve ecstatic escape in the beatific vision. Neither is it the self-sufficient individual secure in his victory through Christ enjoying his own private experience of spiritual gifts and emotional satisfaction. To be saved means to be in authentic relationship with fellow humans under the lordship of Christ. Salvation means that restoration of community which the Old Testament prophets referred to as "the peace of God," and which Jesus referred to as the kingdom of God.

God's goal for human history is the creation of a universal covenant community under God. In the story of Babel the curse of pride and pretension was the disintegration of community and the scattering of the nations (Gen. 11:1-9). This alienation of mankind provides the setting for God's promise to Abraham that all the families of the earth would find the blessing of community in him and his descendants (Gen. 12:1-3). In partial fulfillment of that promise to Abraham, Jahweh saved Israel by calling them into peoplehood. Jesus who came "to save his people from their sins" further fulfilled that prophecy when he called them into community under the peace of God. When they refused his messianic claims, he began the formation of a new disciple community which was completed with the coming of the Spirit at Pentecost. Only within this historical perspective can the excitement and enthusiasm of the new Jesus community at Pentecost be understood.

With the realization that Jesus of Nazareth was truly God's savior to Israel, the first Christians joined themselves in a relationship patterned after the highest community ideal of the Mosaic law. That ideal is to be seen in the provision for a year of Jubilee (Deut. 15, Lev. 25). Every seventh and fiftieth year in Israel was to be a time of restoration. In Deuteronomy 15 it is called "the year of the Lord's release" (see also Isa. 61:1-2, Luke 4:18-19); and it was kept in recognition of their common dependence upon and equality before the God of grace who had formed them into community and given them stewardship of the land. By readjusting the inequities of their economy, restoring the status of those who had become slaves, and living together in trust and joy, they were to proclaim God's salvation in Israel. It was a year of *koinonia* which came to be associated with the final messianic salvation.

Little wonder then that the apostolic response to the fulfillment of God's promise was the formation of a new "Jubilee" community. We are told in Acts 2:42 that those who shared a common Spirit and Lord devoted themselves to the apostles' *koinonia* (community). The baptism of the Spirit was to be found in this new fellowship and not in the old "crooked nation." Here the jealousies and competition of private ownership were overcome in the unity of heart and soul. Here the insecurities and fears were vanquished in the glad generosity of the new devotion to the cause of Christ. Widows and other destitute persons received their fair portion without the stigma of the welfare dole. Here the threat of rejection and a double standard were done away by the gift of the Spirit to each alike. Slaves and women who were ineligible for citizenship in ancient society received the mark of full recognition as persons before God! The shape of God's salvation in Christ was the new *koinonia* under the lordship of Christ through the presence of his Spirit.

It is important not to miss this central point in peripheral arguments about communal ownership in the first Jerusalem congregation. The response of these first Christians was not intended as a blueprint for a communal economy of production and consumption, as may be seen from the fact that other apostolic congregations did not take this form. However, there is plenty of evidence that the *koinonia* of the Spirit continued to provide the dynamic pattern for congregational life. To the church at Philippi, Paul appealed for a community order of servanthood and unselfishness based on "*koinonia* in the Spirit" (2:1-11). To the churches at Galatia and Colossae (Gal. 3:26-28, Col. 3:10-11), he pointed out that to be "in Christ" meant that the barriers of sexual, racial, economic, social, and cultural discrimination are abolished. The religious, psychological, and social distinctions that divide the human community into hostile factions belong to the "old nature." To the Ephesians he wrote that Christ "who is our peace" has created one community out of the old, alienated ideologies of Hellenist and Jew. In his letters to the Corinthian church we learn that sharing financial help was taking place between congregations and across the old cultural and religious boundaries (I Cor. 16:1-4). While almsgiving was also highly esteemed in the Jewish synagogue, more than almsgiving continued among Christians. Service *(diakonia)*, contributing funds, administering aid, and acts of mercy are included among the "gifts of the Spirit" to the church (Rom. 12:6-8, I Pet. 4:10-11, I John 3:17), and generous hospitality remained a sacred duty within the church (I Pet. 4:9, I Tim. 5:10). A new politics of *agape* "which binds everything together in perfect harmony" (Col. 3:14 RSV) had been inaugurated.

Within this new "household of God," this new "chosen race," men and women received their self-identity. "Nobodies" became "somebodies" (I Pet. 2:10). "In Christ" they no longer depended on social roles, economic standards, minority-majority status, religious affiliation, and ideological and political associations to confer individual identity and worth. In the new community of salvation — the body of Christ — identity, dignity, and meaning were given by the Spirit. Those who were alienated and depressed found reconciliation, well-being, and peace as "fellow citizens with God's people" (Eph. 2:18-19 NEB) in a world where only a few enjoyed the status and privilege of citizenship this was a powerful metaphor conveying the meaning of salvation. Within the family of God, wrote Paul, the meaning and goal for living have been disclosed. God's eternal purpose for life, and indeed for all of history, has been made manifest in Jesus Christ, who is the head of this new body (Eph. 1:9-10; 3:7-13). Hope and confidence are restored in the community of his presence.

Reconciliation, acceptance, identity in God's family, new meaning, purpose, and hope — this is the nature of biblical salvation, and the shape of that salvation is the community of God's peace.

Utopia?

Thus far I have argued that the community of salvation is a visible social reality — a historical community of faith and love. But how is it to be identified in history? The paradox of the historical institution called the church and the spiritual, personal reality of which we have been speaking defies easy resolution. Luther attempted to resolve it by equating the saving community with the universal communion of saints. He spoke of the true church as "hidden" and becoming visible only in the acts of personal religious fellowship in the matrix of words and sacrament.[8] Emil Brunner has praised Luther's discrimination in his *The Misunderstanding of the Church*, and offered his own further elucidation: "The *Ecclesia* as *koinonia Christou* and *koinonia pneumatos*, as the Body of Christ, is a pure communion of persons entirely without institutional character."[9] He calls it "the dynamic reality," which finds visible expression in love and fellowship in Christ.[10] In the same vein Paul Tillich equated the true church with the "Spiritual Community," which he called the "dynamic essence of the churches."[11]

While Calvin took the organized congregation more seriously than Luther, he too made a distinct separation between the visible congregation and the invisible spiritual body of Christ to which all the elect belong. Those who are granted supernatural grace, i.e., are "saved," normally express the true faith by participation in a properly constituted congregation, but church membership has little or no organic connection with salvation.

---

8. See, for example, Heinrich Bornkamm, *Luther's World of Thought*, Concordia, 1965, pp. 134ff.
9. *The Misunderstanding of the Church*, Westminster, 1953, pp. 16-17.
10. *Ibid.*, pp. 108-09.
11. *Systematic Theology*, III, University of Chicago, 1963, pp. 149ff.

This same clear distinction continues in the thought of Calvin's evangelical followers.

The problem caused by equating the community of salvation with the spiritual or invisible church is that the ethical tension between visible church and secular world order is inevitably reduced. Salvation and spiritual relationships are relegated to a spiritual body which has a highly ambiguous relation to objective social reality. The ease with which Southern white churches have made sharp distinctions between "spiritual" and "social" fellowship with blacks graphically illustrates this dualism. The spiritual has to do with inner motivation, private intention, and belief. The saved individual continues to live in and according to the socio-political pattern of the temporal order. He does, of course, make moral adaptations to evil practices, but as a "public person" he assumes the validity of the political order. While salvation is claimed as a present experience, its essential benefit lies in a future life after death. The present experience is conceived as justification and inner "peace with God," but there is no new order of *koinonia* to replace the old competitive order of self-interest and private privilege.

Little wonder then that in European and American Protestantism the "Christian nation" has generally been a surrogate visible community of salvation! When the saving community is conceptualized as purely spiritual there is no new social reality within which citizenship can be realized, identity established, and the experienced salvation authenticated.

At the opposite extreme, when the *koinonia* of the Spirit has been equated with a particular historical group, equally serious difficulties have arisen. Two dangers, namely, institutionalism and sectarian exclusiveness, have beset every attempt to identify the true church with a human community. Institutional definitions of the true church make legally authoritative organization the validating mark of the saving community, and, as Brunner points out, define the church as a "corporation."[12] Sectarian definitions tend to delimit the boundaries of the true church according to accepted models of obedience drawn up by the group. Thus not organization but a code of requirements becomes the authenticating mark. In either case the form of legal religion is clearly manifest.

Must we then conclude that there is no resolution to the dilemma? Must we settle for the paradox of *simul justus et peccator* (simultaneously justified and sinner)? Yes and no! No, if that means intentionally settling for one or the other horns of the dilemma. Yes, if it means that we cannot expect a perfect human solution, and therefore the community of salvation itself is understood as a community of grace. The community as well as the individual is saved by grace. The covenant of the saving community is no blueprint for utopia.

The community of the Spirit is not a community of perfection. It is not a monastic attempt to achieve a higher standard of ascetic holiness by self-denial and discipline in obedience to Jesus' "counsels of perfection." Its holiness is not fabricated from its superior obedience, but is given as a consecration under the covenant of peace to which it has pledged loyalty. It dare not follow the sectarian model of the classic Hutterian community and separate itself from the world in an effort to perfect its *agapeic* order. As we have already seen in Chapter 2, it has the character of a movement. Its goal is to be light and salt in the larger societal order. But, and this is the nub of the issue, *it is a community — a social embodiment of the faith, an apostolic fellowship.*

The community of salvation, then, must be more than a sharing of intentions and motivations which express themselves in liturgical fellowship (service to God) and scattered deeds of *diakonia* or service to fellowmen within an alienated, competitive society based upon self-interest. It ought to be conceptualized as more than a platonic sphere or zone of the Spirit's activity which somehow interpenetrates the old structures but does not

12. *The Misunderstanding of the Church*, p. 42.

fundamentally change them. From the biblical teaching we are led to expect a more concrete expression — the incorporation of a new order in the midst of the old. It is a new social embodiment of the Spirit of Christ where everyday patterns of life together enhance the new order of the Spirit.

The intrinsic order of this new redeemed fellowship is *koinonia*. In the New Testament, *koinonia* is variously translated as sharing, fellowship, community, participation, contribution (to the common cause), and communion. It comes from the root *koinos,* which means shared, common, or public in contrast to *idios,* which means belonging to one's self, or private. Accordingly the adjective *koinonikos* means generous, liberal, and sociable. The New Testament pictures an assembly or *ekklesia*[13] of persons who share a common Spirit, Lord, conviction, and mission — a common loyalty signified in baptism, and a shared life. Life is no longer for one's self. That is now recognized for the *idiocy* that it is! Life is life together. Individuality finds fulfillment in a community where persons mean infinitely more than property, where personal relationships are more important than individual achievement, and where individual worth is perceived in the reflection of God's grace, not in the economic utility or social role of the brother and sister. Truly in such communities of the Spirit reconciliation and redemption have begun. They are the "first fruits," the down payment of the Spirit concerning which the apostle Paul wrote.

---

13. The word *ekklesia* denotes a gathering for political as well as religious group action. It is a concrete congregation, i.e., it is a sociological as well as a spiritual reality, and the spiritual realities are given "political" expression in it.

CHAPTER FOUR

The Gospel of Peace

Life in the Spirit is a life of peace. While there are only a few texts in the New Testament that explicitly associate the words Spirit and peace, there is no question that God's present work is to bring peace in the lives of his people. God is called the "God of peace." Christ is the "Lord of peace." The Christian's "walk in the Spirit" is a walk in the path of peace. The fruit of the Spirit is "peace." In a variety of passages peace is immediately associated with joy, righteousness, faith, and love as a prime characteristic of the new community of the Spirit. At least twice St. Paul refers to the good news of Christ as the "gospel of peace," and in Romans 8:6 he writes, "To set the mind on the Spirit is life and peace."

Yet of all these words characterizing the Christian life style none has prompted more explosive conflict among Christians than the word peace. The issues were epitomized in several incidents at a nationwide evangelism exposition some time ago. One of the nearly three hundred exhibitions at EXPLO 72 in Dallas featured the words of Menno Simons:

> The regenerated
> do not go to war,
> nor engage in strife.
> They are the children of peace
> who have beaten their swords
> into plowshares and their spears
> into pruning hooks, and know of no war.

> ... Since we are to be conformed
> to the image of Christ,
> how can we then fight our enemies
> with the sword? ... Spears and
> swords of iron we leave to those
> who, alas, consider
> human blood and swine's blood
> of well-nigh equal value. ...

These words sparked a controversy at the convention. "Peripheral to the gospel," the managers of the convention's exhibition halls argued. The conference, they maintained, had been called to emphasize one thing, namely, the spreading of the gospel, and to raise the question of Christian participation in war was to divert attention to side issues.

Menno Simons was a vigorous sixteenth-century defender of the believers church, the centrality of true conversion, and the necessity of evangelistic preaching, but he certainly would have entered his counter-protest, as did his spiritual sons. Christ, he would have argued, is the "Prince of peace." His kingdom is a kingdom of peace. His Spirit is the Spirit of peace. His gospel is the good news of peace, and his children are to be peacemakers. Peace or *shalom*, to use the Hebrew word from the Bible, is at the heart of the message which Christians proclaim.[1]

Both sides in the dispute proclaimed "the gospel of peace by Jesus Christ" (Acts 10:36). Both claimed allegiance to the Christ of whom Paul writes, "He is our peace, who has broken down the wall which divided us" (Eph. 2:14). On the one side admirals and generals in full regalia unfurled the nation's flag, while thousands of fans cheered for Christ as the "one way." On the other a small, motley band of long- and short-haired advocates unfurled banners reading, "Cross or Flag?" and "God or Country?"

Historically in the Protestant tradition this conflict has tended to coincide with the lines drawn between "liberal" and "conservative." Conservatives have nearly

---

1. Menno Simons, *Complete Works*, Herald, 1956. See, for example, pp. 554-56.

always supported on principle the use of "necessary violence," including war, to maintain the law and order of
the status quo. Yet liberal churchmen too, while they
may have argued pacifism in theory, by and large have
devised a Christian rationale for war when the chips
were down.[2] Today a new alignment has emerged within
both Roman Catholicism and conservative Protestantism. New voices are speaking out. While small groups
like the Mennonites have always challenged war on
biblical grounds, today others within the evangelical
persuasion have begun to challenge the older theological
position from within. They make the Bible the point of
reference for the challenge.

Why the conflict? Evangelicalism has always made
peace a central word in its message of salvation. "Therefore, since we are justified by faith, we have peace with
God through our Lord Jesus Christ" (Rom. 5:1) — this
was a central text of the Reformation and has remained
a favorite word of assurance and comfort for countless
thousands of anxious, burdened individuals who have
found "peace with God." By the sacrifice of Christ we
have been justified and forgiven through faith. Our sins
have been removed as a cause of God's anger and our
own feelings of uneasiness and guilt have been lifted.
That is the classical message of evangelicalism.

But what has this to do with war, riots, and violent
revolutions against political oppressors? Should Christians expect and work for peace *in the world,* or is the
message of peace with God only one of inner, spiritual
tranquility? What did Jesus mean when he told his
anxious followers, "My peace I leave with you" (John
14:27)? In order to understand the nature and significance of the challenge and to find answers to these
questions, we need both the perspective of history and a
review of biblical concepts.

"Peace with God"

During the revivals of the early 1800's, individuals who

---

2. See Ray Abrams, *Preachers Present Arms,* Herald, 1969 (revised
edition).

were in great inner conflict and fear because of their sins often struggled for days in a state of depression and anxiety before they gained peace of mind. Out of this tradition which has colored so much of our religious vocabulary, "peace with God" has come to be practically equated with justification and assurance. Theologically, peace has come to mean that the record of sin and guilt has been properly settled (justification); and psychologically it has come to mean a release from feelings of guilt and a sense of assurance. However, the accentuation of guilt as the central problem in salvation must be traced still further back in the history of Christian thought.

Already in the second and third centuries one can perceive a different emphasis developing between the theologians in the Western or Latin tradition and those under the dominance of the Hellenistic or Greek culture. Latin (Roman) theologians developed those biblical texts which view sin as transgression of law, and salvation as rescue from judgment and punishment. They were heavily influenced by Roman concepts of justice. In the Greek (Orthodox) wing of the church, theologians stressed death as the consequence of sin and salvation as the gift of immortality. While these two emphases were not mutually exclusive, they did produce quite different patterns of piety and theology.

By the tenth century the two traditions had become fixed and largely separated. Within Roman Catholicism, which was the context of Protestant reform, concepts of punishment and just payment for sin were amplified to a high pitch. God, and even Jesus, was pictured as a wrathful judge who condemned the wicked to endless torments of the inferno described so vividly by Dante. At best one could hope for an indeterminate sentence to purgatory. The whole ecclesiastical system of sacraments, pilgrimages, relics, and indulgences aimed at cancelling out temporal and eternal punishments by providing merits equivalent to the demerits of sin.

Luther reacted vigorously against the more legalistic aspects of this system in his search for personal salvation.

Nevertheless he understood the basic problem as one of guilt before God and of the just penalties involved. His struggle was for an inner assurance of God's forgiveness. He wanted a certainty of justification that was not dependent upon any human individual or institution, not even the church. Thus the theological focus remained upon sin as a transgression of God's law, and upon salvation as an individual acquittal before God.

Luther thought that he was simply reaffirming the message of Paul. But while he used Paul's words and in part captured Paul's thought, he was in fact accentuating a different point than Paul did. He used Paul's words to speak to his own problem. The situation in which Paul was writing, as well as the problem that concerned him, were both different from Luther's. It is very important to notice the difference here because Luther's divergence from Paul was exaggerated and perpetuated by the Pietists in the following centuries.

Luther was a medieval man trying to satisfy a stern and angry judge. In contrast Paul said that he had a clear conscience before God even while he was a Jewish rabbi. He was not in quest of personal peace and forgiveness, although when he discovered how wrong he had been, he too recognized that he was greatest of sinners.[3] The great concern which filled his mind was the relation of God to his people. As Paul the Pharisee understood the covenant law (Torah), God's peace and favor were conditioned on obedience to Torah. Israel was living in disobedience and so under the disfavor of God. The problem of restoration to God's favor and the key to messianic fulfillment, as this young, fanatically loyal rabbi saw it, was the problem of Israel's perfect obedience.

Then on the road to Damascus he came to the astound-

---

3. Krister Stendahl says, "Apparently Paul did not have the type of introspective conscience which such a formula [*simul justus et peccator*] seems to presuppose." He notes that Augustine was one of the first to express such a conscience and says further, "In these matters Luther was a truly Augustinian monk." See "The Apostle Paul and the Introspective Conscience of the West," *Harvard Theological Review* (1963), pp. 202f.

ing realization that the Messiah had indeed come even though Israel had not rendered perfect obedience to Torah. Jesus of Nazareth whom he persecuted was the Messiah! And if the Messiah had come, then God had already intervened to bring peace to Israel, not because of the Jews' repentance and faithful obedience but in spite of their disobedience.

It was the implications of this discovery that Paul had to work through in the Arabian desert. *God's peace comes among men as an act of pure grace to be participated in through faith.* God did what Torah could not do because of mankind's weakness. Because of this notable difference of personal and historical context, Paul's concept of "peace with God" is different from Luther's in significant ways.

Without developing the story in greater detail we need simply to note that Luther, the dominant figure of the Reformation, bequeathed this individualistic, spiritualized concept of peace to the Protestant tradition. The Anabaptists, such as Menno Simons, were effectively silenced by persecution. Pietism, which claimed to be the legitimate spiritual heir to the Reformation, put singular emphasis on the individual experience of forgiveness and assurance and the consequent response of personal holiness. Today Protestant evangelicalism perpetuates this gospel of "peace with God."[4] The message of individual peace of mind has become so identified with the biblical message that the rich, multifaceted dimensions of the biblical meaning have been largely overlooked.

Peace — Pax, Eirene, or Shalom?

Peace like heaven is highly desirable largely because the definition is so amenable to individual interpretation. For many peace means simply the absence of war or violence. Others make it almost synonymous with "law and order." Still others think of it as freedom

---

4. This is the title of a volume of Billy Graham's sermons in which the general orientation and point of view I have been describing is represented.

from anxiety and inner turmoil. And for still others it is the absence of confusion or tension in personal relationships. Peace means for them not having disagreements or showing anger.

These concepts derive from an ancient past. The Greeks thought of peace *(eirene)* as a kind of harmony or balance which resulted in stability. Peace was for them tranquility. The ancient Romans from the time of Augustus referred to the *Pax Romana* (the peace of Rome), which was maintained by the power of the emperor's troops. For them peace was a state of "law and order." In this cultural context the New Testament writers spoke of Christ as the true "Prince of peace," and of God as "the God of peace." One can hardly miss the subtle negative inference in Paul's allusion to the Roman *pax* when he says in Romans 14:17 "The kingdom of God... [means] righteousness and peace and joy in the Holy Spirit."

Although the New Testament was written in the cultural setting of the Roman empire and in Greek words, the men who wrote it were of Hebrew background and they brought their own meanings to the words they used. It is almost as if they were translating their Hebrew ideas into Greek linguistic formulas. Because of this it is necessary to look closely at the meaning of the word *shalom* in the Old Testament scriptures in order to understand the meaning of writers like Peter and Paul. The "gospel of peace" is the gospel of *shalom,* and not the gospel of the Greek *eirene* or the Roman *pax.*

According to the prophets peace reigned in Israel when there was well-being, health, justice, equity, prosperity, and good will — when the smile of God's favor was on the land. There was no peace if poverty, famine or disease plagued the land. There was no peace when there was inequity in the distribution of wealth, injustice in the courts, or oppression of the poor. There was no peace when people forgot God and ignored his covenant law which defined the order of peace and righteousness. Thus Jeremiah described the plight of

Israel torn by the sword of her enemies and decimated by plague and famine. Then he uttered the oracle of God, who said, "I have taken away my peace from this people" (16:5). He laments that in this deplorable situation of greed, injustice, and impiety corrupt priests and prophets cry, "'Peace, peace' when there is no peace" (6:14).

In the Old Testament, then, peace is not simply relief from guilt feelings, serenity, or peace of mind. *Shalom* refers to harmonious relationships which grow out of justice and equity in the public order.

This order of righteousness is what God had prescribed in the covenant law. God's law is a "covenant of life and peace" (Mal. 2:5); therefore *shalom* in the public order is also described as the relation between God and His people. In other words, peace has political and economic as well as psychological and religious dimensions of meaning. It is a holistic concept and comes to be almost synonymous with salvation, i.e., God's deliverance from evil, suffering, and sin. Peace is the fulfillment of the covenant promise, and it was this fulfillment which Peter referred to as "the gospel of peace" in his conversation with Cornelius (Acts 10:36).

Given this context, we catch a new insight into the significance of Paul's words in Romans 8:16: "To set the mind on the flesh is death, but to set the mind on the Spirit is *life and peace*." The "mind set on the Spirit" fulfills the "covenant of life and peace" which God has made with his people. The polarity here, as we noted in an earlier chapter, is between Spirit and law as the agent for accomplishing God's covenant purpose. Paul stated this quite explicitly in his letter to the Galatians (5:18): "But if you are led by the Spirit, you are not under the law." To be "led by the Spirit" does not imply that peace has been "spiritualized." Rather the Spirit's power has furnished a new possibility for its realization in the covenant community. Peace is offered as a "fruit of the Spirit."

All this does not invalidate the concept of personal peace with God. Peace as reconciliation and inner confidence is a fundamental part of the biblical message. The inner freedom from conflict which comes through faith in Christ is a basic reality in the Christian's experience, and in fact is another facet of life in the Spirit. What we have seen in the preceding paragraphs, however, is that peace cannot be equated simply with individual justification, freedom from guilt feelings, or inner tranquility.

Peace, then, is a new state or quality of relationship with God and our fellowmen. It opens from God's side a possibility of community bound together by his covenant of justice based on *agape* instead of human justice based upon legally regulated self-interest. In these terms Jeremiah spoke of God's removing his peace from Israel in the face of their stubborn disobedience to the covenant. In the same idiom Jesus said, "My peace I leave with you" (John 14:27) in anticipation of the Spirit's coming and the disciples' obedience to his new covenant and commandment of love.

The Community of Peace

The gospel of peace opens the possibility of a new relationship with God to be lived out in relation with our fellowmen. It calls us to live for the God Movement which, according to Paul, means "justice, peace and joy in the Holy Spirit" (Rom. 14:17 NEB). It is, indeed, the same message which we earlier referred to as the good news of Pentecost. It is the announcement that a new community of God's peace has been established by the Spirit, and that an invitation to join the new community or movement has been issued.

"In Christ," as we have seen, we are called to a relation that transcends national loyalties, language barriers, sexual difference, racial distinctions, religious suspicion, social class, and economic rivalry. Christ "who is our peace" has "brought us together" in a way that no political figure could ever do. He has broken down the barriers to peace. For those who have been raised with Christ the old mores and etiquette, status symbols, religious and cultural taboos, national ideologies, and standards of living no longer determine the structure of community relationship.[5]

It is important to note that these categories of change "in Christ" are social, legal, political, and economic. They have to do with more than attitudes and intentions of the heart. They speak to the structure and character of the human community under the rule of God. They are not simply "spiritual" or religious ideals which we have no real responsibility to carry through. The "in Christ" position is not a haven of mystical satisfaction and tranquility but a new moral and social possibility in the community of God's peace.[6]

Far too long the dominant religious tradition in America, sometimes called WASP, has been content to preach a gospel of "spiritual" peace and brotherhood that does not fundamentally affect the social structure of our lives. According to this "gospel" military personnel can wreak indiscriminate death and destruction with the peace of God in their hearts. Lily-white congregations can enjoy "spiritual" kinship and peace with black Christians who would be unwelcome to the fellowship in person. Popular evangelists living in relative luxury spend millions of dollars to preach spiritual "peace with God" to people caught in the impossible and soul-destroying trap of poverty and disease without lifting a finger to help. Preachers and laymen alike join in the political game of denouncing street riots in the name of peace while attempting nothing to alleviate the unjust, frustrating conditions which sparked the violence. Indeed, to even raise these issues in the name of evangelical witness is to be called peripheral, disruptive, and naive. There has been a blackout in the "city set on a hill."

The message of peace, therefore, comes first to the church, calling it to again be the prophetic community demonstrating the peace of God in the midst of compe-

---

5. See Col. 3:10-11; Gal. 3:27-28. We have dealt with these passages in Chapter III.

6. See Eric H. Wahlstrom, *The New Life in Christ*, Muhlenberg, 1950. This Lutheran scholar has challenged the application of categories such as "Christ mysticism" to Paul, and makes a solid case for the moral character of the "in Christ" idiom.

tition and violence. As the community of the Spirit it is exhorted to bear the fruit of the Spirit, which is "love, joy, peace..." (Gal. 5:22).

The essential form of the community of peace is found in the new *koinonia* that was initiated at Pentecost. The first congregation at Jerusalem, "filled with the Spirit," instinctively moved to fulfill the highest precept of commonality found in the Torah of Moses, the "year of the Lord's release," or the "year of Jubilee" (see Deut. 14:28-15:11 and Lev. 25). According to that law the earth and its wealth belong to God, and therefore that wealth was to be distributed according to the needs of God's people. The land was not to be sold "in perpetuity" (Lev. 25:23). To make allowance for human failures, periodic redistributions were to be made, culminating in the "year of the Lord's release" every fifty years. At that time debts were to be cancelled, family properties lost by misfortune were to be returned, and in general the poor were to have a chance to even the score and begin anew.

This law was never fully obeyed under the old covenant. Gradually the imbalance of poverty and wealth increased, and conditions that led finally to Israel's collapse and captivity developed. Thus the idea of such a time of God's favor came to be associated with the messianic rule, as we see in Isaiah 61:2 and in the Magnificat (Luke 1:51-53). Jesus himself recognized and underscored the validity of Isaiah's prophecy when he quoted it in the synagogue at Nazareth to describe his own mission (Luke 4:18-19). He had come, he said, "...to proclaim the year of the Lord's release." So the community that formed at Pentecost on the confession that Jesus was Messiah immediately moved in the spirit of Jubilee to distribute their wealth according to the needs of all concerned, and reestablish the peace of God.

We are not called upon to take this instinctive expression as a literal blueprint for organizing the church, but the fundamental spirit and form of the new community of peace are clearly and forcefully enunciated. Two opposing principles of organization are explicitly named.

The one is *koinos* or commonality. The other is *idios* or individualism. We are told that no one said of his possessions, "They are *idios*"; but they held their possessions *koinos* (Acts 4:32). Two spirits are strikingly portrayed. The one is a spirit of openness and sharing — not in the sense of "charity" but as an act of fair play and justice. The other is a spirit of privacy and self-interest.

This first Christian congregation organized its life on the principle of commonality of interest and the conviction that the individual self can find realization and fulfillment only in the shared experience of the reconciled community. This is in striking contrast to the social-contract theory upon which our democratic society today is based. The contract is assumed to be between private competitive egos, and is based on the principle of enlightened self-interest and a balance of power.[7] These are two different and conflicting concepts of peace; and the one based on *koinonia* is the essence of the New Testament.

The Anabaptists of the sixteenth century who sought to take this vision of the New Testament church seriously were called perfectionists and "heaven stormers."[8] Today "naiveté" and "socialist" seem to be more effective epithets. In light of this we must stress that no single economic or political plan is being suggested as a blueprint of the kingdom. No definitive pattern has been or will be devised by man to perfectly organize the peace of God. No legalized formulas can or will ever fully express the Spirit of *koinonia*. What is seriously amiss in the life of American evangelicalism, however, is its defection from the *koinonia* principle and its identification of private property (*idios*) and the balance of enlightened self-interest with the New Testament ideal. Starting from this assumption, it has failed through the years to take seriously the mission of peace and

---

7. The "social contract" was spelled out by the English philosopher John Locke as the only way to regulate the selfish interests of men. In place of authority which is based upon despotic power he advocated enlightened self-interest.

8. This term meant they were striving to get to heaven by good works.

justice which Jesus himself proclaimed and committed to the church.

The faithful church also directs the message of peace to "the principalities and powers," to those in positions of public authority and responsibility. Those in public office also stand under the law of the God who disclosed himself in Christ. The peace of God proclaimed by Christ and his apostles, as we have seen, is not a purely individual matter. In the final *epiphany* (manifestation), Christ will be revealed as "Lord of lords" — i.e., Lord of those exercising public authority. Under the rule of Christ the peace of God will not be imposed by arbitrary might, but by intrinsic right. "The rod of iron" is not a rod of despotic, arbitrary power! *And this intrinsic right even now lays claims upon governments and all public powers.* Even though "the kingdom of God and his righteousness" are not yet fully vindicated, the church proclaims its conviction that they are even now the ultimate standard of justice and peace.

The easy assumption of two ethical standards — one for the believer's private life and one for public policy and action — has played havoc with the church's witness to the Lordship of Christ. It has led to accommodation and support of the political status quo with the plea that nothing more can be expected of the secular state. It has allowed Christians in control of business and industry to justify admittedly sub-Christian standards of operation in their company activity while carefully maintaining a high personal morality. But even more seriously, it has in a kind of reflexive thrust led to accommodations with worldliness within the church itself. Fellow members of Christ deal with each other according to the patterns and norms set for secular social institutions. The democratic process has become the formula for peace. Even in the church it is each man for himself. *Koinonia* has been transformed into camaraderie and "auld acquaintance."

The message of peace must be a word spoken by a faithful church to remind the government and other centers of power that their authority is not their own but God's and that therefore their exercise of power stands under the judgment of Christ who is the final revelation of God. That is true now, not only in the age to come.

Finally, the gospel of peace calls the church to *peace-making*. The God Movement is a *shalom* movement, and a peacemaker is one who works for the movement. (I have used *shalom* for peace because the word peace, like love, has become vulgarized, and in order to make the point here, some precision of meaning is required.) Jesus said, "Blessed are the peacemakers," and we have generally assumed that he meant the arbitrators, reconcilers, and possibly even the truce-makers and pacifiers. Perhaps in its broader sense it may include all those who work for peaceable solutions to human conflict. But more precisely a "peacemaker" is one who works in and for the God Movement to bring about *shalom*.

The hallmark of Christian peacemaking is the ministry of reconciling men to God (II Cor. 5:20-21). As we have seen in Chapter 3, this means initially bringing men into the revolutionary community of peace under the lordship of Christ. For the mission of peacemaking we must have volunteers who have first made peace with God and themselves. Nothing less than a radical conversion from *idios* to *koinonia* will do. They must, as Jesus said, "be born of the Spirit."

This Holy Spirit of *koinonia* is the spirit of *agape* that casts out the fear and insecurity which cause men to clutch their possessions. It is the spirit of gratitude that in Christ all things belong to us so that we are freed from competition and possessiveness. It is the spirit of contentment and reconciliation to life or death because Jesus Christ is Lord of both. And perhaps we should also be explicit about what it is not. It is not the spirit of *asceticism*, which rejects the goodness of material things in order to achieve perfection. Neither is it the spirit of *mysticism*, which despises the goods of this life as opposed to the spiritual. Nor is it the spirit of secularistic *communism*, which demeans individual worth in the name of group values and goals. Spiritual birth introduces a genuinely new revolutionary quality in life.

Only when we begin to understand the radicalness of Christian peacemaking can we understand the absolute necessity for radical conversion. The mission of peace is a "mission impossible." It confronts the worldly establishment with the offensive announcement that in Christ God has made its wisdom foolishness (*moronic* in the Greek) and its power weakness. And it follows this pronouncement with the politically naive call to find peace through the way of the cross. (See I Cor. 1:18-25.)

Christian peacemakers operate on three principal convictions which are disclosed through the prophetic tradition of both the Old and New Testaments. The first is that the world and all in it belongs to God. This revealed axiom stands in direct contrast to the human assumption that the wealth of this world is the private property of individuals who have a right to use it for their own self-aggrandizement. The second is that all men share equally in God's loving concern. This contrasts with the pagan assumption that in his inscrutable providence God has shown favoritism to some men and nations.[9] The third is that *koinonia* is the formula for peace. Because we share God's love equally, sharing God's wealth is a principle of justice. This stands in sharp contrast to the assumption of power politics that the formula for peace is justice based upon the balance of competitive self-interest.

Based on these principles, the ministry of peacemaking inevitably leads to an identification with the poor and the downtrodden. Peacemakers heal the sick and wounded, free the slaves and imprisoned, feed the hungry, and care for the rejected and lonely. They also work for the vindication of God's kingdom and his justice.[10] Peacemakers are those who "hunger and thirst to see right prevail" (Mt. 5:6 NEB).

---

9. This was an explicit assumption of the Puritans and other early settlers in America and was used to justify taking the land from the Indians and enslaving the Blacks. It has remained implicit in the arguments of the sons of the Puritans to this day.

10. A. M. Hunter suggests that we might paraphrase the fourth beatitude: "Blessed are those who ardently desire the vindication of

In the light of this it is obvious that men and women who have caught this new vision of God's rule of peace can never again be uncritically loyal to their old fatherland. They are now citizens of a new "holy nation" under a new authority and working from different presuppositions (I Pet. 2:9-10). They dare not on pain of disloyalty to their new government conform to the patterns of this age (Rom. 12:1-2). Competition, status-seeking, selfish accumulation of wealth, violence, discrimination, injustice, impiety, and the like are simply intolerable to the renewed mind.[11]

In Western Christendom the evangelical churches have become so identified with the national self-consciousness that they have failed to see the radical implications of nonconformity at the systemic level. The ethical principle is almost entirely applied to personal matters such as use of alcohol, illicit sexual behavior, and attendance at "worldly amusements." Ironically it took a Hindu saint reading the Christian New Testament to reintroduce the importance of "noncooperation with evil" at the systemic level.[12]

Peacemakers will always need to confront the secular system with noncooperation (nonconformity), because that system is essentially based on the principle of competitive self-interest. There seems to be confusion about this among Christians today. In many minds democratic freedom has been virtually equated with freedom in Christ.[13] The democratic process has been identified with justice; and peace which is legally imposed by a ma-

---

the right, and triumph of the good cause." He also suggests the same meaning for the word "righteousness" in 6:33. See *A Pattern for Life,* Westminster, 1953, pp. 34, 81.

11. The popular notion that Christian nonconformity applies only or even primarily to the individual's private morality — smoking, drinking, dancing, and sex — is a travesty on the radicalness of the New Testament.

12. Gandhi taught that noncooperation with evil which dominates in human society is just as important as cooperation with the right.

13. Carl McIntire's *Author of Liberty,* Christian Beacon Press, 1946, is an extreme but consistent example of this kind of thinking. John Foster Dulles, as the architect of the policies of "containing communism," is still revered by many as the great *Christian* statesman of this century.

jority has been equated with the peace of God. On these assumptions it is simply taken for granted that the *Christian* way to work for peace and justice is to "work through the system for orderly change."

While we must appreciate the democratic system, and may on many occasions work through the political process, we must also keep clearly in mind that secular democracy is based upon the *self-interest of the majority* and not on justice as such. It is to be hoped that this majority will be enlightened with a sense of justice, but Christians should never confuse the "justice" of the majority which is written into statutory law with the justice of God's kingdom. Peacemakers live not by majority opinion but by the new law of Christ. Their life style reflects the way of peace; and their nonconformed presence in the world as strangers confronts and sensitizes the public conscience.

The God Movement introduced a revolution into the affairs of men, and revolutions are never quiet affairs without stress and strain. Jesus himself said, "I am come to cast fire upon the earth...." And again he said, "I did not come to bring peace but a sword." Paul and Silas were described as men who turned the world upside-down. In an evil world peace can never mean the quiet of withdrawal or accommodation. The Movement aggressively promotes the peace of God as central to its evangelical message and task.

It seems appropriate to end our chapter as we began it with words from Menno Simons' tract on *The New Birth:*[14]

> This regeneration of which we write, from which comes the penitent, pious life that has the promise, can only originate in the Word of the Lord, rightly taught and rightly understood and received in the heart by faith through the Holy Ghost.

*   *   *

> These regenerated people have a spiritual king over them who rules them by the unbroken sceptre of His mouth, namely, with His Holy Spirit and Word.... His name is Christ Jesus.

14. *The Complete Writings of Menno Simons*, pp. 93-94.

They are the children of peace who have beaten their swords into plowshares and their spears into pruning hooks, and know war no more. They give to Caesar the things that are Caesar's and to God the things that are God's.

Their sword is the sword of the Spirit, which they wield in a good conscience through the Holy Ghost.

*   *   *

Their kingdom is a kingdom of grace, here in hope and after this in eternal life.

Their citizenship is in heaven, and they use the lower creations with thanksgiving and to the necessary support of their own lives, and to the free service of their neighbor, according to the Word of God.

CHAPTER FIVE

The Spirit of Love

If peace is the message and mission of the community of the Spirit, its inner quality and dynamic is love *(agape)*. In the previous chapter we examined the concept of peace as a right pattern of relationships with God and our fellows. Now we must look carefully at the love that motivates and guides the community in its quest for peace. This "love of God poured into our hearts through the Holy Spirit" is the truly revolutionary characteristic of the God Movement.

We have, in fact, reached a crucial point in our examination of the God Movement. We have seen that the "peace of God" calls for a radical change in human relationships, and that the followers of Christ are to aggressively promote this radical change. Like Paul and Silas of old, they should be turning the world upside-down. Is this simply another idealistic appeal to violence for the sake of establishing peace? If it is not—and it is not—then the secret must lie in this spirit of *agape* which informs both the character and method of the peace revolution.

Karl Marx, father of the modern Communist revolution, is quoted as having said, "My goal is to change the world." At his best Marx was interested in justice and equity. In some respects he reminds one of the Old Testament prophets who cried out in anger against the rich oppressors. But Karl Marx's method for bringing about such a revolution was force and violence. He was convinced that the wealthy bourgeoisie would never give up their privilege by choice. Therefore he taught that they must be overcome by violent revolution. And as we are all well aware, this basic assumption has led modern Communism to justify violence and intrigue, exploitation and oppression as legitimate means to bring about a revolution of peace and justice.

Jesus too was interested in a revolution of peace and justice, but in diametrical contrast to Marx, Jesus taught that the only method which could bring about true peace and justice is love.

In the story of Jesus' temptations we are told that Satan offered him three popular ways to be a successful revolutionary leader. First, he suggested that he use miraculous power to make bread and feed the people. The suggestion is that if Jesus could promise the hungry multitudes food, he could then command their allegiance. He might be a benevolent dictator. In the second temptation Satan suggested that Jesus come as a great religious leader and miracle-worker. Through the show of supernatural power he could impress the crowds and become a great authoritative leader. When Jesus rejected this suggestion, Satan made his last appeal, namely, that Jesus worship at the feet of force and violence. The tempter showed him all of the "kingdoms of the world" and claimed that it was within his power to give them to him. Jesus could gain power as the Caesars had gained it — through war and violence. As they had imposed the "peace of Rome" on the ancient Near Eastern world in this manner, so he could impose at last the true peace of God.

In all three cases Jesus rejected these demonic substitutes to the way of the cross. His revolution was to be radically new. It was to be the revolution of *agape*.

Eros, Philia, and Agape

The whole law is summed up in the word love, Paul wrote to the Christians at Rome (Rom. 13:10). And Jesus had also said that love to God and one's fellows are the greatest commandments, comprehending the whole intention of the Law (Mt. 22:37-40). Unfortunately, however, the English word love has become so ambiguous because of its many possible meanings that we must find a more specific term to carry its Christian meaning. What kind of love fulfills the Law? What kind of a "new commandment" has Jesus left for his disciples? The Greek language contains three words which can be translated love. Each one has its own distinct meaning, and the writers of the New Testament use one almost exclusively.

First there is the word *eros*, which means desire. The moral quality of *eros* is determined by the nature of the object desired. When the object is good then *eros* is virtuous. When it is illicit then *eros* is lust. *Eros* itself is neither good nor bad. It is essentially a passion or impulse aroused by an object which seems desirable. It is a strong motivator toward action which will satisfy the craving, whether it be for God, knowledge, or some less worthy object.

Eros is the dynamic for all social relationships based upon self-interest. Advertisers, politicians, and educators all attempt in one way or another to manipulate or condition desire so that their projected goals may be achieved. Political philosophers have argued that in the long run the greatest good for the largest number will also be good for each individual, and that therefore we ought to desire the good of the majority. National leaders attempt to persuade their fellow countrymen that altruistic aid to less fortunate countries is in their own best interests, and they often explicitly reassure them that the government will do nothing which is not in the national self-interest. Advertisers persuade the public that one brand of bandaids or cigarettes satisfies more than the rest. Educators purvey knowledge as the means to man's highest end. Human society is rooted in self-interest and motivated by *eros*.

The second word for love in the Greek language is *philia*, which denotes the mutual or reciprocal relations of friendship. This is the love of camaraderie and mutual trust. It is, as Aristotle long ago pointed out, the very basis of political community and even of family solidarity. Cooperatives and mutual insurance societies are good examples of such reciprocal helpfulness in the world of economics. The United Nations is an extension of *philia* from the local and national level to the level of world relationships.

Philia is really a variety of *eros*. It is enlightened self-interest based on prudent trust. *Trust* is the new element, but it is a trust conditioned by trustworthiness and mutuality. Notice the two elements of prudence: A friend must gain our confidence, i.e., we must have reason to believe him worthy of confidence. But further, the benefits of friendship must go both ways. There is an intrinsic element of pragmatism in *philia*. Whether consciously or not, *philia* calculates the advantages of friendship for itself.

Eros is never used in the New Testament, and *philia* is not prominent, although these were the words most commonly used in classical and Hellenistic Greek. Perhaps it was precisely because the word *agape* was so nondescript and unused that the early Christians made it their word. That way they could fill it with their own newly found meaning. *Agape* describes the kind of love disclosed in Jesus Christ. As John says, "It is by this that we know what *agape* is: that Christ laid down his life for us" (I John 3:16).

Agape has a unique quality that goes beyond both *eros* and *philia*. It is not a response to the desirable, lovable, or admirable but to the needy — the undesired and unloved. Its essence is revealed not in the response to a friend but to an enemy. *Agape* seeks to create a loving response in the unloving. It initiates action when prudent self-interest does not necessarily dictate such action. *Agape* acts unilaterally! It accepts the burden of vulnerability because it respects the other person and always hopes for the best. That is why the supreme symbol of *agape* is the cross.

Such action is not only difficult in the doing; it is difficult in the conception! So much that we have manufactured in the name of Christian *agape* has in fact been tainted. Whether our concepts have shaped our actions or merely described them *de post facto,* the church has by and large reduced *agape* to charity or benevolence. At least since the days of Charles G. Finney and the "benevolent empire" built on the evangelical revivals of the 1830s, evangelicalism has accepted charitable altruism or benevolence as the working definition for *agape.* In effect we have based our life in the community of the Spirit on the principle of *philia,* and have urged sacrificial altruism as a counsel of perfection. But, and we must say it emphatically, *agape is not benevolence!*

In his critique of the new morality the late Bishop Pike called attention to this definition of *agape* as benevolence and rejected it as an adequate basis for Christian ethics.[1] He pointed out that when one "loves the unlovely and unlovable" he is implicitly and inescapably "belittling" the beloved object. "For it [*agape* — benevolence] to be recognizably operative it is intrinsically requisite that the other be assessed as unlovable, unworthy, undeserving, *no good.*"[2] Pike's criticism was aimed immediately at Joseph Fletcher's "situation ethic" based on love, but it applies equally to all systems that equate *agape* and benevolence. He has exposed the worm in the apple of much Christian charity.

In the teaching of Jesus the object of *agape* is not the unworthy person but the *enemy.* "Enemy" like "friend" describes how I view the other person. It is a projection of my feelings of fear and threatenedness onto that person. If there are also feelings of unworthiness, they are

1. While Pike's critique is aimed principally at Joseph Fletcher, who equates *agape* and benevolence, he notes that the identification of these two is very widespread. It is important to note the precise use of words like "unlovable" and "unlikable" as the object of *agape.* That is quite different from making the object the *unloved* and *undesired.* When benevolence makes the former its object there is an inescapable element of condescension and belittling in it. As Pike says, "It supplies a sense of goodness and well-doing to one person while *belittling* the other." See *The Situation Ethics Debate,* edited by Harvey Cox, Westminster, 1968, pp. 198-99.
2. *Ibid.,* p. 199. Taken from *You and the New Morality,* Harper and Row, 1967.

just that — my *feelings* projected onto the object. Fear turns an opponent, real or imagined, into an enemy. *Agape* transcends fear and hostility, enabling the one who loves to see and respect the worth of an enemy. As John put it with beautiful simplicity, "Perfect *agape* casts out fear" (I John 4:18).

The essential nature of *agape* became evident only when God revealed the unique and inalienable worth of all mankind in the incarnation. A person's worth, from the Christian perspective, does not depend upon education, wealth, sex, nationality, race, or ideological convictions.[3] It has nothing to do with his immediate value to me for my ends in life. *Agape* takes self and self-interest out of the center as the prime measure of the other's worth.[4] It recognizes the worth of the other person as one beloved and esteemed of God in spite of any real or imagined threat that person might pose to me. *Agape* is not a response of charity to the unworthy but of good will to the enemy and friend alike. It is God's love which indiscriminately sends rain and sunshine on the just and unjust.

While *agape* implies selflessness in the sense of not being selfish, it does not imply self-rejection. It no more requires the "belittling" of oneself than of the other! Only those who know God and stand confident of their own worth in his love are strong to love as He loves. This was the beauty and strength of Jesus himself. Fully aware "that he had come from God and was going back to God," he became the servant whose service dignified and enhanced the lives of those whom he served (John 13:3-4). And he called his followers to such *agapeic* service.

It may be obvious by this time that love leads to action. Love is a verb before it becomes a noun. Love is love as it expresses itself in *koinoniac* action. We are

---

3. II Corinthians 5:16. "With us therefore worldly standards have ceased to count in our estimate of any man" (NEB).
4. This is the meaning of Jesus' words, "Let him deny himself." The word translated "deny" really means "lose sight of self," so the passage might be better translated, "Let him stop looking at things from a selfish perspective."

not to love "in theory and talk but in deed and truth," wrote John. And he pressed his point with the rhetorical question, "But if a man has enough to live on, and yet when he sees his brother in need shuts up his heart against him, how can it be said that the divine love dwells in him?" (I John 3:17-18).

Love as Identification

Agape is redemptive involvement in the sin and suffering of the world. We have come to know *agape* in God's incarnation, in his becoming a man among men, sharing our lot, making himself a servant incognito, and bearing our hostility and sin in order to create a response of love in us. In this same way the world comes to know God's love through our expression of his love in action.[5]

Richard Keithan, a long-time missionary to India, told how a non-caste peasant once threw himself at his feet in a posture of worship. The action was intended as an expression of gratitude for the genuine concern which Keithan had shown to him. Keithan, however, was somewhat embarrassed and a bit irritated that one man should pay such worshipful respect to another, and he pulled him to his feet saying, "Get up. I am not God." Not to be rebuffed, the Indian peasant replied, "Yes, Sahib, but we never saw God until you came." God's *agape* had been expressed through his servant, and had found its mark.

But we must say more. *Agape* is involvement of a distinct kind. There is a definitive quality or character which distinguishes it and has implications for the way in which the church is to be involved in the life of the world.

Agape seeks involvement through *identification* with those whom it seeks to serve. Jesus himself identified with "the poor." In contrast to the Pharisees, who said, "This multitude is accursed because it knows not the

---

5. See John 17:18 and I John 4:12. These verses clearly suggest that we now stand in the same relation as the earthly Jesus did in making known God's love.

law," Jesus had compassion upon the crowds because they were "as sheep without a shepherd." There are many examples which illustrate Jesus' ability to identify with the person to whom he related. He ate with publicans and sinners. He conversed with women, even with a Samaritan woman and with prostitutes. He earned the reputation of a "drunkard" because of his close association with the lower classes in their way of life. He made the cause of the poor his own and offered them first place in the God Movement.[6]

This does not mean that he rejected or despised the rich. Neither does it mean that he sanctioned uncritically the motives, purposes, and goals of the masses. Indeed, it is very clear that he did not. But it does mean that he took the side of the oppressed against the oppressor. Both the poor and the affluent ruling class recognized this. To the rulers his identification with the poor was a threat. To the poor themselves it was their ground of hope.

In order to understand the significance of *agapeic* identification, we must contrast it to the paternalistic altruism against which Jesus warned his disciples.[7] Paternalistic aid is inherently condescending. It assaults the self-respect of the person whom it attempts to help. It demands, whether covertly or openly, that the recipient recognize the right of the benefactor to his superior status and power, and therefore his right to control the use of what he has donated. At the same time, it expects a recognition of the donor's goodness and therefore gratitude properly expressed in submission and humility.

Such an assumed right is entirely foreign to *agape*. The example of Jesus as described by Paul in Philippians 2:5-8 is the model. He laid aside his "God form" and took the "servant form." This was the essence of his *emptying* himself. In order to do this, he completely assumed the "likeness" of a man among men — a man

---

6. Luke 6:20. Also see the discussion of this point in chapter 6.
7. Luke 22:25. "The kings of the Gentiles exercise lordship over them; and those in authority over them are called benefactors. But not so with you. . . ."

without status or power. He was born a Jew among Jews, a peasant among peasants. He could not "pull his rank" because he had no rank to pull. Such is the identification of *agape*.

Today we are witnessing a worldwide revolt of the have-nots (now called the "Third World") against the paternalistic imperialism of benevolence. The restless poor are asserting their right to live their own lives and to run their own programs of improvement without outside paternal interference and control. Even secular government is aware of the new demand. It is trying to find ways to distribute welfare aid that will not discourage initiative or demean self-respect.

The words of Jesus against paternalism were never more appropriate for the Christian church. Following from its understanding of *agape* as benevolence, it has, with the best intentions, identified with the affluent and served the poor and the pagan from a position of paternal strength. It has ministered to the poor, but has seldom been the voice of the poor. It has run programs *for* the poor in order to improve their conditions and status — which improvement, of course, has been defined in its own terms. Even in its program of evangelism, the church has not acted as one beggar sharing good news with another, but as the rich man lifting the beggar out of his misfortune.

Identification implies respect for the other person and understanding of his situation and feelings. At its best this is the *agapeic* meaning of mutuality in love. According to the standard of *philia*, mutuality is a calculation of reciprocal ability to render service. But *agapeic* mutuality calls for *koinonia* — fraternal relationship and responsibility which rests not on mutual ability to reciprocate but on an *agapeic* identification with the person in need which makes him neighbor and brother.

Jesus illustrates this dimension of *agapeic* mutuality in the story of the Good Samaritan (Luke 10:25-37). Following an interchange in which Jesus said that the first and second commandments were to love God and "your neighbor as yourself," a lawyer asked him, "Who is my neighbor?" Who am I mutually responsible to love as myself? That was the question.

The lawyer was, of course, aware of the canons of mutuality and friendship, and to his legalistic mind this was a perfectly proper question. How do you define neighbor? According to the standards of *philia,* a neighbor would be defined as one who reciprocates in mutual ties of respect, responsibility, and friendship. Such ties of responsibility were formed by familial, religious, or national relationships — Romans to Romans, Jews to Jews, Galileans to Galileans. But Jesus said in the stark clarity of the parable that *agape* makes *every man in need* a neighbor. *Agape* obligates me not to an act of altruism as a paternalistic benefactor, but as a brother for whom a mutual debt of assistance is obligatory without further ado.

Certainly this is the basis for understanding the aphoristic advice of Jesus in the Sermon on the Mount. When Jesus said, "Give to him who asks of you, and lend without expecting it to be paid back to you," he was not encouraging an irresponsible, impetuous charity which can be as demeaning of persons as paternalism. Rather he was recommending that generous spirit which recognizes a brother-neighbor in everyone who has need and which accepts *agapeic* responsibility for him.

In obligations of *agapeic* mutuality no questions are asked about the worthiness of the one in need. The needy person is worthy because he is accepted as brother. No questions are asked about his ability to reciprocate. It is enough to have been privileged to befriend a neighbor. The service of *agape* is an end in itself because it fulfills the very meaning of humanity both in the giver and receiver. It is its own intrinsic reward.[8]

Agapeic identification applies even to the enemy. It assumes the burden of his misunderstanding and hostility. Undoubtedly the unfortunate Jew on the road to Jericho would have despised and rejected his benefactor

---

8. The persons who "gave the cup of cold water in the name of Christ" were not conscious that they had done anything deserving of reward (Mt. 25:37; see also Luke 17:19).

in other circumstances — "the Jews have no dealings with the Samaritans!" But the Samaritan did not bother to inquire into the Jew's attitudes or to use them as an excuse. *Agape* bears the burden of proof in such a case. It seeks out need even in the face of antipathy and rejection, and finds a way to serve as neighbor.

Agapeic Justice

At first blush it may seem strange to speak of a loving justice. In the Western Christian tradition, Roman Catholic and Protestant alike, love and justice have been contrasted, and love has been associated with mercy and grace. While justice is identified with morally equivalent punishment — "an eye for an eye, and a tooth for a tooth" — love as mercy pleads for forgiveness. When justice is considered as a standard for distribution of goods, it is generally defined as a minimum one might rightly expect. Love then is conceived as grace which goes beyond the minimum and gives more than is deserved. This is the "plus" of benevolence or charity.

As we have noted earlier, the theological rationale of Protestantism has been heavily influenced by these concepts and definitions. Sin is a transgression which incurs moral guilt, and justice is the equivalent penalty which matches the quantity of guilt incurred. Love, then, as mercy and grace, is disclosed in Christ who paid the just penalty for the offense. Indeed, some popular lay theologies in this tradition have called Christ "the Greatest Criminal," the one who pays the penalty of all criminals.[9]

The language of penalty, just retribution, and mercy does not logically require associating guiltiness with worthlessness. But historically in orthodoxy the concept of moral *guilt* has in fact subtly come to imply moral *unworth* and *lack of moral value*. The notion of personal offense has been translated into the language of

---

9. I do not intend to argue for or against the penal theory of atonement in thus stating the bias of evangelicalism. However, a redefinition of terms would inevitably result in some modifications. The point here is the conceptualization of love and justice that lies at the heart of all orthodox theology.

moral debauchery and unworthiness, and *agape* has thus been understood as God's response to the unworthy — the nobody and the no-good. Accordingly, justice provided for behavior toward persons based upon their actual worth (the merits of the case) ; and love defined as grace dispensed with the category of worth or merit on the assumption that the recipient was actually unworthy. In either case worth was calculated according to the rules of *philia* — worth to society, worth to me. The great human temptation is to reduce all relationships to the level of *philia,* where they can be dealt with in political and psychological business as usual.

The idea that man as sinner has less worth stems from St. Augustine. Implicit in his concept of the "fall of man" and "original sin" is the loss of a constitutive element of human goodness and value. When the change resulting from the fall is given a quantitative, ontological value, it is almost impossible to avoid a negative valuation of the sinner as a defective person — or so it has proved in the history of Christian theology.

This is a fine point but an exceedingly important one because it marks a watershed between a Christianity that accommodates itself to the old politics of *philia* and *eros* and the new community of *agape.* The offense against goodness is real and has moral consequences. Offense causes pain and hostility. It is destructive of personal relationships and of personal character. For these reasons the offender may properly be called "offensive" and guilty, and such guilt must be taken care of if the damage is to be repaired. God has taken sin very seriously indeed! But here is the crux. By the standards of *eros* the offender is not only unloved and undesired but also undesirable and unlovable. By the canons of *philia* he is unworthy of friendship. But divine *agape,* while acknowledging the full weight of the offense, persists in recognizing the offender's dignity and his worthiness of reconciliation. This recognition of the worth and right of the offender is the *agapeic* basis of justice.

Deserving of forgiveness? Does that not contradict the very concept of God's grace? Not necessarily; it only enlarges it to include God's creative as well as redemptive activity. In the incarnation of Christ, God revealed that creation itself is an act of *agape,* and that therefore grace is not simply a redemptive response to things gone wrong. *Agape is grace bestowing worth in the very act of creating a person.* If this were a volume of systematic theology, we might enlarge upon the theological implications of this view. Here we only note its implication for the mission of the church. When the community of God's Spirit makes *agape* the formative principle, its ministry of reconciliation will be motivated and informed by a spirit of moral justice rather than charitable altruism.

The message of *agape* is that God does not view the human situation in terms of *philia* — not even in its most exalted moral sense, where friendship goes out of its way to show benevolence and grace. There is no condescension in *agape!* From the divine point of view, perishing mankind is worth saving. Restoring the relationship broken by sin is worth the painful reconciliation. Precisely that is the revelation of love in Jesus Christ.

Agape introduces us to a world of relationships in which forgiveness is a matter of justice — "God is faithful and *just* to forgive us our sins" (I John 1:9); in which even if we are asked to forgive our neighbor seventy times seven times in a single day, we are to do it simply as a matter of duty — "We have only done our duty" (Luke 17:1-10 NEB). It is a world in which "just deserts" are not tallied up like wages for hours worked — "Thus will the last be first, and the first last" (Mt. 20:1-16). Under the new law of *agape* one is morally bound to "go the second mile" and to "turn the other cheek." The highest measure of justice in the God Movement is expressed in vindicating the helpless and showing mercy to the poor. In one word *agapeic* justice is *koinonia.*

It is important to realize that *agape* is not a "counsel of perfection" for individuals to emulate. Rather, it is the spirit and essence of life in the community of the Spirit. *Agape* is the standard requirement of the law of Christ. Obedience to this new law gives no one special status. Neither is it an impossible (or unrealistic) ideal which always judges and forgives our necessarily imperfect attempts to reach it. *Agapeic* justice is the "new righteousness" which provides the organizing principle for the community. It provides the moral basis for the new politics of love. Indeed, we have not and do not perfectly fulfill it, but that is not because it is an impossible principle which can only be approximated in a lower standard of natural justice.

To speak of *agape* as a spirit and attitude does not answer the hard questions of how such a *koinonia* is to be organized. What has been attempted here is the more modest task of writing a prologue to the politics of *agape*. By the same token what has been criticized is not the human failure of the church to perfect an *agapeic* system. Rather, it is its failure to recognize the radically new character of *agape* and to acknowledge that it is indeed the standard for organizing the life and mission of the church.

The church as one of the institutional "orders of creation," to use Luther's concept, has assumed that the order of natural justice tempered by love is the formative principle of its life. Thus operating within the definitions of Western capitalistic society, it has assumed that the "sacred right of private property" justifies the accumulation of excessive wealth when it is earned in accordance with the economic and legal canons of the system. For all practical purposes stewardship has been defined as giving a tithe, and charity has been conceived as spontaneous altruism and "sacrifice" rather than as the obligation of justice. (*Agape* has generally been associated with spontaneity and feelings of compassion and pity.)

In the area of criminal justice, the church has by the same token justified and supported the state's definition of just penalty even to the extent of capital punishment. It has at most asked that justice be tempered with mercy. The concepts of prisoners' rights and of incarceration as correction and rehabilitation have come largely from the secular disciplines of social work and social psychology.

Even now, the weight of evangelical opinion supports concepts of criminal justice based upon the rational and political structures of *philia*.

By the same token Roman Catholic and Protestant orthodoxy has supported the validity of war, only asking that it be "just." It is interesting to note that the definition of justified violence has largely ruled out the violence of the exploited against those systems which rule and exploit them. Justice has usually been biased in favor of the established order, and in Western Christendom the church has been part of that order.

But the heretical definitions and assumptions of *philia* have been most devastating in the missionary crusade of the church to Christianize and civilize the "heathen."[10] (The argument between those who espoused evangelization rather than Christianization concerned only the methods of approach. The evangelist fully expected his converts to adopt the patterns of a "higher" civilization.) The very word "heathenism" denoted inferiority, and the "sacrifice" of the missionaries was described openly in the language of condescension. Funds to run the enterprise were collected as charities for which the home churches expected gratitude as well as conformity to their wishes. The mission was often imposed on the basis of imperialistic violence — implicitly if not explicitly.[11]

---

10. See Robert Handy, "The Christian Conquest of the World," in *A Christian America: Protestant Hopes and Historical Realities,* Oxford, 1971, pp. 117-54.

11. It is common knowledge that the great missionary advance of the eighteenth and nineteenth centuries was based upon the imperialistic expansion of Western nations. That the guns of American soldiers opened the way for the gospel has been victoriously avowed from many a pulpit. Even now many evangelical leaders justify wars against Communism on the grounds that missionary activity will be curtailed if the Communists win the struggle. This is more than a tacit admission that the missionary enterprise has been based on violence. For example, the following appeared in a recent release by the Area Secretary for Southeast Asia of the Christian and Missionary Alliance to all Official Workers in North America: "May I encourage you to continue in prayer for the situation [Viet Nam War]. The outcome of a communist take over of South Viet Nam would undoubtedly be that both Cambodia and Laos would quickly succumb to communist elements. Thailand would probably opt for either a pro-communist stance, or perhaps a neutralism similar to

I must pause again to make clear that this is not a criticism of individual missionaries who gave their lives for the sake of Christ. Most of the Christian missionaries were persons of the highest caliber and integrity. They served with genuine compassion and concern. In many cases the Spirit of love was genuinely manifest in their ministries in spite of the assumptions, organization, and methods of the missionary enterprise. But the time has come for us to recognize that the theological and ethical rationale of American Protestantism[12] is seriously inadequate to provide a self-understanding and strategy for the decades ahead.

The *agapeic* mission is motivated by the simple fact of man's need and God's love which obligates me to my neighbor. "For the love of Christ," wrote Paul, "leaves us no choice.... His purpose in dying for all was that men, *while still in life, should cease to live for themselves*" (II Cor. 5:14-15 NEB). The incarnation furnishes the model of identification with the life and culture of those to whom *agape* is directed. Again, in the words of Paul, *agape* becomes "all things to all men." Its service "in the name of Christ" attaches no strings. In short, its purpose is to reconcile men to God and their fellowmen, not to spread a Christian civilization throughout the world.

---

that found in Burma. In either event, it would likely signal the end of Christian missionary endeavor. *I cannot believe that it is in God's providence or purpose that an additional fifty-six million people be sealed off from free access to the message of the gospel....* [Italics mine]

This was in a letter of thanks for the "wholehearted cooperation and support on the day of fasting and prayer called for May 7, 1972," which at the same time reported the stabilization of the situation in South Viet Nam and new optimism that the war could be won by the South.

12. I have used Protestantism instead of evangelicalism because the situation described applies equally to evangelical liberalism, as Robert Handy's historical description makes abundantly clear. Nevertheless it is evangelicalism as it has emerged from the older fundamentalism that now attempts to continue the missionary enterprise with renewed enthusiasm on the basis of the old, inadequate concepts.

CHAPTER SIX

The Witness to Grace

In Chapter 2 we referred to the church as a "propaganda ministry for the God Movement." Now in this concluding chapter we will explore further the implications for evangelism of what we have learned about the community of the Spirit.

We have noted that the gospel message is that promise has now become reality in Christ. We have not argued that the reality is consummated. The salvation so beautifully symbolized in Revelation by the "holy city Jerusalem coming down out of heaven from God" (21:2-22:5) remains a hope for the future. However, a significantly new stage has been initiated in which Spirit displaces law as the guide and dynamic of the saving community. Paul succinctly described this reality as "the power of God unto salvation" (Rom. 1:16).

We have observed that the reality of salvation as it is presented in the New Testament includes more than the life, death, and resurrection of Jesus. Pentecost and the birth of the church also belong to the gospel. The new *koinonia* of the Spirit is the community of reconciliation within which salvation is experienced. It is the community of grace formed under the new covenant which we enter through repentance.[1]

---

1. *Metanoia*, the New Testament word for repentance, means a complete readjustment and reorientation of our lives. It is far more than expressing sorrow for past mistakes.

97

This same community which exists "by grace through faith" is also the *community of witness*. We have seen that it has the character of a movement always remaining in and for the world. Jesus described it as a "city set on a hill" whose light beckons and guides the weary, lost traveler to the security and camaraderie of a civilized society.[2] In the city there was safety from the marauders who took advantage of the darkness to rob and kill. In a friendly city a foreigner could find protection and hospitality. Thus Jesus used the city as a symbol of the saving community whose light shines in the gathering darkness, inviting the traveler to find salvation.

It must be obvious that this coalescence of the community of grace and the community of witness implies not only an integral relationship between propaganda and reality but also between the message and the method of evangelization. In the well-known phrase of Marshall McLuhan "the medium is the message!" The *koinoniac* form and the *agapeic* spirit are both message and medium simultaneously. Indeed, this coalescence of method and message is implicit in the word *witness*. A witness is not someone who repeats what has been told to him, or someone who has learned a technique of communication. He is someone who has experienced (witnessed) the reality which he reports as a testimony (witness). He is one through whom the love of God becomes known to

2. I have used the word community throughout the essay, but the word city *(polis)* would be almost equally acceptable if we understood the connotation of that word for the ancients. The city was the center of civilized life. It was the symbol of political order, where life was humanized. It was the center of commerce and therefore abundance. Behind its walls was security against invaders. Thus it early became a symbol of God's work in history as well as of the achievement of man in defiance of God. We are told that in contrast to the wealthy cities of ancient Chaldea Abraham looked for a city built by God (Heb. 11:10; cf. 12:22). Revelation 18-21 describes the final destruction of the city of Babylon (man's city) and the descent of the heavenly city in glorious beauty. Within that city, whose twelve foundations symbolize the twelve apostles, flows the river of life beside which stands a tree of life on either side. The light of this city is Christ himself and "by its light shall the nations walk." This is simply a highly symbolic description of the community of salvation.

others because it has become a reality in his own life (I John 4:13-21) .

Perhaps the major problem in our contemporary practice of evangelism is the breach between message and method. The wistful words of one student from India doing graduate study in the United States should haunt our consciences. He said, "I could never become a Christian because I respect the teaching of Jesus too much." Our example and method (reality) had invalidated the message for him.

The inconsistency between method and message is most evident at two points: First, in the virtual reduction of evangelism to verbal communication, and second in the use of manipulative techniques to achieve conversions. The emphasis upon the past ("once for all") reality of Christ's work has focused our attention on doctrine and verbal communication. Evangelism has been practically equated with speaking the word, and with a special mode of speaking at that. Evangelistic manuals tell how to ask leading questions; find the right verses; memorize the correct succession of spiritual instructions; or saturate the community with religious literature. The way of salvation has been reduced to "five easy lessons" in doctrine, and faith is conceived as belief that such doctrine is true. To a large extent we have disassociated salvation from the present reality of a caring, sharing, renewing community.

Secondly, the church has followed too readily the lead of the Madison Avenue managerial professionals in the use of manipulative techniques which create desire and then satisfy that manufactured desire. Taking our cues from modern advertising, we have too often turned witnessing into a massive persuasion campaign. Technique and image have been substituted for relationships and reality. The same point may be put another way. In one evangelism workshop I attended a speaker used the figure of scratching where it itches. "Christians who want to witness for Christ in the world," he said, "should scratch where it itches" — should meet need where it is felt. One participant responded, "Yes, but

suppose it does not itch where you think it ought to."
This concerned Christian, like many of his equally concerned brothers, had perceived evangelism as a means
of producing conviction — a sense of need which his good
news could then relieve.

It is of the utmost importance that we rediscover a
method of gospel witness which itself will enhance and
commend the message of the New Testament.

The Method of Jesus

While there is no reason to make a fetish out of Jesus'
methods, there does seem to be good evidence that his
command to the seventy disciples reported in Luke's
Gospel represents a general guide to witnessing. In
chapter 10, after giving a series of specific instructions
which we may regard as local in time and place, Jesus
said, "Whenever you enter a town and they receive you,
eat what is set before you; heal the sick in it and say to
them, 'the kingdom of God has come near to you'"
(vv. 8-9).

Three imperatives stand out in this commission: First,
Jesus told the disciples to *eat* what was set before them.
Second, he commissioned them to *heal* the sick; and
last, they were to *tell* the people that God's kingdom
was near. If we paraphrase these imperatives into a more
formal methodology, we might say first *identify* with
the people; second, *demonstrate* the reality of God's
power; and third, *announce* the gospel.

Even before we look more carefully at this formula,
we must pause to notice that it clearly moves from non-
verbal to verbal, not vice versa. The movement is from
attitude to action and then to verbal announcement.
One cannot help noting that the current pattern of most
evangelistic missions moves in the opposite direction.
While there is no reason to insist that this formula be
literally followed in every situation, nevertheless there
is good reason to believe that it is a sound principle of
communication, and that it is consistent with the message itself. Certainly it was the apostolic pattern. The
message of the apostles was winged with power by the

51420

demonstration of the new reality of the Spirit at work among his people. These demonstrations were "signs" of the new reality, and they stopped the voice of opposition — though not the opposition itself (Acts 4:21-22).[3]

We need not verify this point with an exhaustive reference to all the New Testament evidence, but two different types of illustration may be cited. Luke reports that in the Jerusalem church during the weeks that followed Pentecost, "the apostles gave their testimony to the resurrection of the Lord Jesus" with "great power" (4:33). This statement is sandwiched within a description of the new *koinonia* which demonstrated the power of the Spirit among the apostolic band. The apostles' reports about the resurrection of Christ had convincing power because everyone could see a demonstration of the living body of Christ! The reality authenticated the witness.

The second illustrative passage is I Corinthians 2:4-5, where Paul contrasts persuasive speech, eloquence, and wisdom in the preaching of the gospel with the "demonstration of the Spirit and power." There is nothing in these early chapters to suggest that this "demonstration of the Spirit and power" simply refers to the emotional impact of his words through some inner enduement of the Spirit. The power of the Spirit was creating at Corinth a new community of love in the midst of individualism, rivalry, and self-centered religious ecstasy. It was a body in which Jesus Christ was recognized as the "source of . . . life . . . wisdom . . . righteousness . . . consecration and redemption" (1:30-31).

According to Jesus' commission the evangelist is to

---

3. The charismatic movement is again emphasizing the relation of experience and power to witness. The charismatics accentuate the spiritual *power of the message itself*, which is not the power of rhetoric or logic. For example, Rodman Williams says of Peter's speech "immediately" after the outpouring of the Spirit, ". . . his speech was not the same as before Pentecost. It was now laden with power — spiritual power. It was not great oratory or 'enticing words of man's wisdom,' but it was in 'tongues of fire' lighted by the Holy Spirit." We must note, however, that the stress of the charismatics is upon an *individual* experience of enduement of the Spirit's power. See *The Pentecostal Reality*, Logos, 1972, p. 94.

Lincoln Christian College

begin by identifying himself with those to whom he would communicate. In the world of Jesus and the apostles, eating together indicated a bond of appreciation, respect, and acceptance. One of the major complaints against Jesus was that he ate with sinners — with tax collectors (collaborators with Rome), common artisans and peasants (the unclean), and worse, even with prostitutes and drunkards. One of his most serious offenses was his intimate association with the poor who were "accursed" because they did not know the law (John 7:49). Jesus justified himself by saying, "I came to call sinners not the righteous to repentance." One of the first lessons the Jewish Christians needed to learn was that they should eat with Gentiles. Jewish scruples forbade this, but the new order required new respect for persons of all cultures and religions. Even the "barbarians," that class to which Aristotle accorded less than full human status, had dignity.

To identify with another means to *accept* and *affirm*. This does not necessarily mean always to agree with. While Jesus identified with the poor and championed their cause, he frequently reproved them for selfishness, lack of faith, and the like. Affirmation indicates the ability to see past cultural, moral, or other differences to the worth and self-respect of the other person. Jesus saw in the vacillating Simon a rock, in the quiet Nathaniel "an Israelite in whom there is no guile," in the weeping prostitute a woman who had loved much. He affirmed them for what in their best moments they most wanted to be.

Acceptance of the other one is perhaps most concretely expressed in the admission of our own need of that person. Jesus himself exemplified this acceptance of others in his constant dependence upon them. He asked the Samaritan woman for water, to her surprise and delight. In a striking public act of acceptance, he invited himself to the home of Zacchaeus for dinner. He constantly relied on his friends, using their boats and homes, eating their food, enjoying their companionship.

He needed them! That is the authenticating mark of a real incarnation.

The authentic witness to grace must give up self-sufficiency and independence. That is the inner meaning of Jesus' command to go without provisions and accept the hospitality of the people to whom one would witness. How much of modern witness at home and abroad has gone out from a secure cultural and economic base which allowed the evangelist autonomy and distance. Such autonomy in method contradicts the message of incarnation.

We need not belabor the point that an evangelist must demonstrate the reality he preaches. Jesus himself spent much time and energy healing diseases, feeding the hungry, exorcising demons, and forgiving sinners. In the words of Cleopas, he was indeed "a prophet mighty in *deed* and *word* before God and all the people" (Luke 24:19b). He promised his disciples that they would also receive power to do even greater deeds than he had done, and so it was. (John Calvin's explanation that the signs of God's power are no longer necessary since Christendom has been established looks suspiciously like an excuse, although he was undoubtedly sincere in his belief.)

In the context of "identification" and "demonstration," the verbal announcement will take the form of an *explanation* and *invitation*. We might paraphrase Jesus' words to the seventy as follows: "Exhibit the reality of the kingdom through action before you talk about it." Just as example should precede advice, so questions aroused by observation should precede the evangelistic answer. Jesus' own example will serve here. By his extraordinary ministry he raised the question of his messianic identity long before he attempted to explain to his disciples who he was. Similarly Peter's sermon at Pentecost was a response to the questions of the crowd aroused by what was happening.

Again, we are not pressing for a literalistic following of these precedents, but the relationship of act and explanation in evangelism is absolutely essential. The

262.73
K91
5142

role of a witness is not argumentation and debate. He must depend on more than the cogency of logic or the power of rhetoric. His final appeal cannot be to some authority to certify his claim. Neither dare he rely on the compulsion of mass suggestion. Only the authenticity and winsomeness of example and the actuality of the healing, reconciling presence of the Spirit can validate the witness.

Finally, the proclamation always implies an invitation. The gospel is like the announcement that dinner is ready. That means come and eat! Like an announcement of graduation, a wedding, or the opening of a new business, it always has an implicit RSVP. It is a call to leave the old and join the new community of the Spirit. And the form of the invitation is "Come and see." Such an invitation gives authenticity and credibility to the message.

3 4711 00183 7832